MW01098790

NATURAL WONDERS

OF OREGON

NATURAL WONDERS

OF OREGON

Archie Satterfield

COUNTRY ROADS PRESS
Oaks • Pennsylvania

Natural Wonders of Oregon:
A Guide to Parks, Preserves & Wild Places
© 1996 by Archie Satterfield. All rights reserved.

Originally titled *Green Guide to Oregon*. Updated, with additional information.

Published by Country Roads Press
P.O. Box 838, 2170 West Drive
Oaks, PA 19456

Text design by Studio 3.
Map by Allen Crider.
Illustrations by Dawn Nelson.
Typesetting by Typeworks.

ISBN 1-56626-150-3

Library of Congress Cataloging-in-Publication Data

Satterfield, Archie.
    [Green guide, Oregon]
    Natural wonders of Oregon : a guide to parks, preserves
and wild places / author, Archie Satterfield ; illustrator,
Dawn L. Nelson.
        p.   cm.
    Previously published as: The green guide, Oregon. © 1993.
    Includes bibliographical references (p. 88) and index.
    ISBN 1-56626-150-3
    1. Natural history – Oregon – Guidebooks.   2. Oregon –
Guidebooks.   3. Natural areas – Oregon – Guidebooks.
4. Wildlife refuges – Oregon – Guidebooks.   I. Title.
QH105.O7S38   1995
508.795 – dc20   95-7287
                                                                       CIP

Printed in the United States of America.
10   9   8   7   6   5   4   3   2   1

To the late Ray Atkeson,
who introduced me to so much of Oregon's beauty
while helping start my writing career

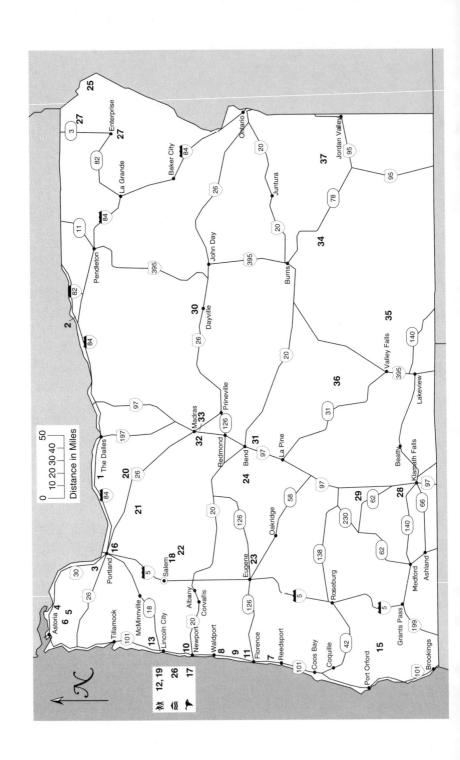

Distance in Miles

0 10 20 30 40 50

Contents

Introduction

Several years ago, at my constant urging, one of my sisters and her family moved from Missouri to Oregon's Willamette Valley, and their experience reminded me of why I moved to the Pacific Northwest so many years ago. At first they were reluctant to believe that a place could be so nice. The valley had the four seasons they had enjoyed in the Midwest, including groves of oaks and other trees that turned colors in the fall and put forth delicate leaves in the spring. But they were most impressed, I think, with what Oregon didn't have; things they could easily live without: poisonous snakes, tornadoes, regular hailstorms, severe cold and severe heat, and humidity so heavy it almost could be sipped.

They also found that most Oregonians recognize the value of their surroundings and have a long reputation of protecting their scenic, benign land from overdevelopment. They have been pioneers in environmental protection legislation intended to keep the state a pleasant place in which to live and continue to try to protect their beautiful state from being "loved to death" by well-meaning but uneducated newcomers.

Oregon has been a national leader in this awareness of our environmental heritage. The state's forestry practices laws are considered the best in the world by many governments, and they have been copied and adapted by other states and many foreign governments. The so-called Bottle Bill, requiring deposits on bottles and aluminum cans, was controversial when it became law, but Oregonians are justifiably proud of the bill and wouldn't think of changing it. The proof of its value is the almost total lack of bottles and cans along Oregon's roadsides.

Another victory, which came about almost by accident, was the state's acquisition of nearly all of its coastline. Without this public ownership, the entire coastal area could easily be lined with ticky-tacky motels and gift shops, fast-food joints, and muffler shops. Instead, you can find miles and miles of natural landscape, and acre upon acre of unobtrusive state parks and federal preserves.

Although this book is called a Green Guide, it doesn't preclude the inclusion of Oregon's desert, where green is usually limited to lawns, green lichen, and interstate highway signs. Oregonians are proud of their desert, which occupies much more land than the evergreen forests and valleys west of the crest of the Cascades. In fact, many residents are as well versed in the history and ecology of the desert as they are of the Willamette Valley. They revel in the differences within their state's boundaries.

This book should be considered only an introduction to Oregon's green places. Hefty tomes have been written about where to hike and camp. The Bureau of Land Management, which oversees much of eastern Oregon, has published two thick volumes about wilderness areas worth preserving in the desert and in the mountains east of the Cascades.

I hope this book will not only encourage readers to visit Oregon's green places but also help with efforts to set aside additional areas for our perpetual enjoyment.

To help clarify road designations, I've used the following abbreviations: I=interstate; US=US route or highway; and State= state route or highway.

1
Columbia River

COLUMBIA RIVER GORGE NATIONAL SCENIC AREA

It isn't nearly as deep as the Grand Canyon or Hells Canyon, nor is it lined with mansions like the Hudson River is, but the Columbia River Gorge remains one of the most scenic – and most approachable – canyons in North America. Fortunately, it was designated a National Scenic Area before it was "loved to death" by home builders, assorted businesspeople, and loggers.

This 292,000-acre protected area stretches about eighty miles from Portland east, almost to US 97. Governmental control has been controversial from its inception because many local residents feared the designation would adversely affect their economic welfare. In the case of loggers and land developers, it *has* cost them jobs and income. On the other hand, it has boosted the tourist industry.

The scenic-area designation protects the canyon and limits growth to existing urban areas. Adopting the designation required tribal governments, counties, the forest service, and a gorge commission to jointly draft a management plan to protect the scenery while developing outdoor recreation. The fact that these groups, who usually fight among themselves, were able to accomplish the plan is something of a democratic miracle.

Incredibly beautiful, the gorge is special for a number of reasons. To begin with, it has more than 100 waterfalls – the Oregon side alone has 77, including Multnomah Falls, the 620-foot grandfather of them all, with a trail to the top and a beautiful footbridge mid-level. Other memorable waterfalls are Horsetail, Oneonta, Wahkenna, Fairy, and Bridal Veil.

Each visitor soon adopts one of the falls as his or her special place, and Oneonta is high on the list of favorites. It isn't one of the highest but it provides an intense feeling of intimacy. Oneonta is at the end of an extremely narrow canyon with walls that seem to almost touch above your head as you tap-dance up the streambed from rock to rock until you reach the punch bowl below the falls. The creek has carved a gracefully curved lip in the softer rock, which looks as though it could have been designed by a Japanese landscape architect. Photographers should be aware that the gorge is so narrow that sunlight hits the stream, and the waterfall itself, for only a brief time each day.

Competing as the most photographed site is Crown Point and Vista House, as seen from the viewpoint at the Portland Women's Forum State Park.

Not only does the gorge have stunning natural scenery, it also has one of the most beautiful and carefully built highways in America. The original Columbia River Highway was started with private money before World War I and officially opened in 1916. The designer, Samuel Lancaster, was taken to Europe by Sam Hill, the highway's principal sponsor, to study highway-building techniques in the Alps. Thus, the seventy-three-mile Columbia Gorge Highway is one of the few examples in America of a highway as artwork. To a great extent Lancaster succeeded. The highway has many touches of Old World elegance and charm reminiscent of castles, including elaborate stone bridges, vaulted tunnels, and guardrails.

Years later when I-84 was under construction and a roadbed was blasted at river level, the old highway was ignored; consequently, some of it was destroyed and one of the tunnels was dynamited shut. With the scenic-area designation bringing more attention to the area, the Oregon Highway Commission has committed itself to restoring the highway to its former glory by the year 2000.

By driving as much of the old highway as possible, you will gain more of an appreciation for the gorge's spectacular beauty than by staying in the fast lane on I-84. The highway begins just east of Portland at Troutdale and originally ran all the way to Hood River. Only segments of it survive today, but there's enough left to give you a choice of driving the older highway in one direction, with its unpretentious small towns, and the interstate in the other. Another popular route is to drive around Mount Hood with stops in the Mount Hood National Forest for hikes, camping, or a picnic.

The scenic area, plus Badger Creek Wilderness, Mount Hood Wilderness, Salmon-Huckleberry Wilderness around Mount Hood, and Columbia Wilderness above the gorge behind Bonneville offer a wide selection of wilderness experiences within an hour's drive from Portland.

The forest service has about a dozen campgrounds along the gorge and the state has parks of all sizes, some only large enough for a few picnic tables and others with RV and tent sites. Spotted randomly along the way are several smaller nature preserves, some owned by the Nature Conservancy and similar organizations that prefer not to publicize them so they won't be overused.

One characteristic of the gorge is the strong winds that blow through it nearly constantly because it is the only corridor through the Cascades. This steady wind and the slackwater behind the series of dams make the gorge a perfect place for wind surfing. Seldom are you unable to see wind-surfers dressed in wet suits, flitting across the river like demented butterflies, darting around the barges and towboats that use the river as a highway.

Another wind-borne phenomenon is the winter storms imported from east of the Cascades, where the weather is much colder in the winter — and hotter in the summer. Sometimes these winds bring in ice storms, which are called "silver thaws."

The gorge has no cities, only small towns that range from one-store metropolises to those with up to 50,000 residents. On the eastern slopes of the Cascades you will find numerous orchards — beautiful both in the spring, with their aromatic blossoms, and again in late summer, when the fruit hangs heavy on the branches.

Dozens of trails lead off from the gorge, some along creek beds that end abruptly at the foot of a cliff. Others zigzag across the face of the gorge until they arrive at the top, with views in all directions. Occasionally, a trail will head far back into the mountains, almost requiring rock-climbing experience, but these are as seldom as roads with a gentle grade.

No matter what activity you pursue along the river, you

probably will be most aware of the gorge itself because its brooding beauty overpowers everything else around it. Late in the afternoon the blue mountain peaks fade off into the distance, resembling a scene in an Oriental painting. The waterfalls are so perfect that some look like they were arranged by a clever movie-set designer. The large towboats, pushing four or five barges through the slackwater pools behind dams, bring the romance of the sea hundreds of miles inland. Even though you may resent the chain of dams that turned this wildest of rivers into a series of lakes, the Columbia Gorge still has a sense of wildness about it, which is one of the reasons the scenic-area designation was established.

For more information:

Columbia River Gorge National Scenic Area, 902 Wasco Avenue, Suite 200, Hood River, OR 97031. 503-386-2333.

Mount Hood National Forest, 2955 N.W. Division, Gresham, OR 97030. 503-666-0771.

Oregon State Parks, 525 Trade Street S.E., Salem, OR 97310. 503-378-6305 or 800-452-5687.

Wind and weather information: 503-386-3300.

UMATILLA NATIONAL WILDLIFE REFUGE

This refuge in the desert along the Columbia River was created in 1969 as something of an apology to wildlife enthusiasts and conservationists for the construction of John Day Dam. The lake behind the dam raised the river level about twenty-five feet, destroying the rich wildlife habitats that had flourished along the riverbank and on the islands.

The flooding, however, wasn't a complete environmental disaster because it also created wetlands in the desert, and these marshes made excellent replacement habitats. Since the refuge was created, the Army Corps of Engineers — who regulates the dam and Lake Umatilla behind it for navigation, flood control, irrigation, and power generation — works closely with the refuge staff to maintain water levels for the maximum protection of fish and wildlife in the area.

Some of the younger residents at Umatilla

About half of the refuge's 29,370 acres, straddling both sides of the Columbia, are farmed to provide food and cover for wildlife. It also adds color to the essentially tan and brown landscape along this stretch of the Columbia River. Among the crops grown are corn, sunflowers, wheat, alfalfa, and wheatgrass. The fields are burned or mowed, usually in the spring, to stimulate growth so the new crops will be available for the waterfowl. Burning and mowing also help control undesirable weeds, such as purple loosestrife, yellow star thistle, Canada thistle, and Russian knapweed.

The refuge is a prime nesting area for Great Basin Canada geese and several species of ducks. Waterfowl populations may reach 300,000 mallards and 30,000 Canada geese during the fall and spring, which is when the most visitors arrive as well. About 90,000 Canada geese and 200,000 ducks winter over at the refuge, creating a terrific din with their conversations and filling the sky with wings when they lift off, turn, and whirl before settling back again. The Canada geese produce about 1,000 goslings each spring. The largest number of ducks ever counted was 458,000 on November 13, 1983.

If you like eagles, a good time to visit the refuge is during the fall migration, when bald eagles come to feed on sick and injured birds. The most counted thus far were 71 immature and 22 adult eagles. Other birds include long-billed curlews, once a favored source of meat for Oregonians, and the small burrowing owls who take over abandoned badger dens. In all, more than 180 species of birds have been recorded at the refuge.

Mule deer, coyotes, muskrats, raccoons, porcupines, and beavers also are found on the refuge. Rattlesnakes have been seen, but they are not common.

The refuge is in an area of extreme desert climate. During the summers temperatures over 100 degrees are common for several consecutive days, and in the winter it can drop well below zero. The six to eight inches of annual rainfall occur during the autumn and winter months. Consequently, photographers can expect clear weather in summer, but bring a bottle of water: the climate and temperature are definitely desert.

About 138,000 persons visit the refuge each year, which is open from 5:00 A.M. to 10:00 P.M. year-round. Some sections are closed from October through June to protect the nesting birds, and a few parts are never open to the public. Numerous parking areas have been placed along the refuge's road system, and hiking is permitted in all open areas.

Only nonmotorized boats may use the refuge ponds and impoundments, where you'll find good fishing for walleye, crappie, and bass. Steelhead and salmon are sometimes found there, and an occasional sturgeon.

The refuge parallels I-84 and is near Irrigon, Oregon. It has several access roads off the freeway.

DOUGHBIRD

The long-billed curlew is North America's largest shorebird and was once known as the "doughbird" because it tasted so good. It tasted so good, in fact, that it was one of the most popular of all game birds. Around the turn of the century hunters shipped wagon loads of them down the Columbia River and sold them for a nickel each.

As with all national wildlife refuges, hunting is permitted during the usual seasons so you will probably want to plan your visit accordingly.

For more information:
  Umatilla National Wildlife Refuge, U.S. Post Office Building, Sixth and "I" Streets, Umatilla, OR 97882-0239. 503-922-3232.

SAUVIE ISLAND WILDLIFE AREA

When the Lewis and Clark party was drifting down the Columbia River in November 1805, on the last leg of their voyage to the Pacific Ocean, they were in a hurry to reach their destination before winter set in. Thus they failed to see the mouth of the Willamette River, for they went on the north side of an island which blocked their view of this major river. It was in this area that Native Americans introduced them to the wapato root, later named arrowhead, so when they found the Willamette River on their return trip the following spring they named the island Wappato. It is the largest in the Columbia and had long been the summer home for the Multnomahs.

The name didn't last; a few years later it was renamed for Laurent Sauvie, a French Canadian employee of the Hudson Bay Company at Fort Vancouver, who operated the company's dairy on the island. After the Hudson Bay era ended, American settlers took over and turned the upstream end of the island into something of a Portland suburb, and so it remains, to a degree, today. During Prohibition, farmers earned extra money with their moonshine. According to local legend, one farmer also made a good income pulling automobiles out of a mud puddle near his farm. The treacherous puddle was there because every night he replenished it with buckets of water, ensuring that it remained a quagmire.

Even after the area filled with people, most of the downstream end of the island was left as marshland and sloughs. It also remained a resting and breeding ground for migratory waterfowl, and in 1947 the Oregon Department of Fish and Wildlife began acquiring land to protect this habitat. By the 1990s the wildlife area had grown to more than 12,000 acres.

Established primarily for wintering waterfowl, the island supports several other species of wildlife in addition to the ducks, geese, swans, and sandhill cranes. Bald eagles are a common sight, as are great blue herons. In all, more than 250 species of birds inhabit Sauvie Island and 37 species of mammals have been counted, including raccoons, red foxes, and black-tailed deer. The painted turtle, which has yellow lines on its head, is among the twelve species of amphibians and reptiles that also live on the island. An interesting note about swans: They pluck vegetation from around their nests for fifteen feet in all directions to create a moat. Potential predators must cross this, and by doing so, they come into full view and are vulnerable to the swans.

More than 1,000 acres are cultivated to provide winter food for the wild residents. Corn, millet, buckwheat, and grains are grown there, and livestock are permitted to graze in the area to remove old forage and to stimulate new growth.

To reach the refuge from Portland, take US 30 west. About ten miles from downtown Portland, cross the Sauvie Island Bridge over the Multnomah Channel and follow the signs past the private property of the upstream end to the refuge land. Users must buy either an annual permit for $10.00 or a daily permit for $2.50.

For more information:

Oregon Department of Fish and Wildlife, 2501 S.W. First Portland, OR 97207. 503-229-5403.

Sauvie Island Refuge, 503-621-3488.

LEWIS AND CLARK NATIONAL WILDLIFE REFUGE

As the Columbia River nears the ocean it becomes broader and moves slower, and its heavy load of silt begins dropping to the bottom, constantly adding acreage to a maze of islands along the Oregon side. The river here is flooded twice daily by the incoming tide, which is so strong that it reverses the river's current. Only a few islands are high enough to escape flooding, and they are generally classified as tidal swamps, with their growth of willows, dogwoods, an occasional Sitka spruce, marsh grasses, mosses, and weeds.

The other islands are not much more than marshes and sandbars, alternately covered and uncovered by the tidal flow and seasonal flooding. The temporary nature of these islands and their swampy character discourage human use, so wildlife has them mostly to themselves.

Dozens of the islands have been formed on the Oregon side of the river upstream from Tongue Point on the outskirts of Astoria, and they are favorite resting places for migrating waterfowl and year-round residents alike. In 1972 the islands were turned into a

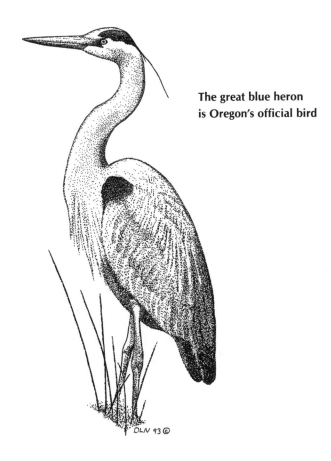

The great blue heron is Oregon's official bird

wildlife refuge that now covers about 35,000 acres of islands, sand-bars, mud flats, and tidal marshes.

The refuge stretches from Welch Island across from Skamo-kawa, Washington, to Tongue Point. Downstream from here the river deepens and the scouring action of the tides and current pre-vents islands from forming. Welch Island is separated by a shallow waterway from Tenasillahe Island, which is part of the Julia Butler Hansen Natural Wildlife Refuge for Columbian White-tailed Deer in Washington.

The Lewis and Clark refuge provides habitat for up to 3,000 tundra swans, 2,000 Canada geese, and 50,000 ducks during the peak migration period of February and March, when the birds assemble before the last push of their migration back to the Arctic. It also protects many species of fish — coho, chum, and Chinook salmon; steelhead and sea-run cutthroat trout; and white sturgeon — that use the shallow waters for spawning and feeding, and as a route from the ocean to the upper reaches of the Columbia.

Fisheries biologists have found that juvenile salmon feed here while going through the physiological changes that enable them to survive in salt water. Other fish that use the area include shad, smelt, perch, starry flounder, bass, catfish, and Pacific lamprey. Harbor seals, California sea lions, beavers, raccoons, weasels, mink, muskrats, and sea otters, are present as are, of course, the Colum-bian white-tailed deer on the upstream islands near their refuge.

The islands are accessible only by boat. Launch sites are at the mouth of the John Day River near Tongue Point, at Aldrich Point near the upstream end of the refuge across from Skamokawa, and at Skamokawa.

NUMBERS GAME

Six species of fish commonly called trout live in Oregon's 385,000 acres of standing water and its 28,000 miles of streams. The species are rainbow, cutthroat, brown, brook, Dolly Varden, and lake. In spite of this common usage, the latter three actually belong to the group of fish known as chars.

For more information:

Lewis and Clark National Wildlife Refuge, c/o Willapa National Wildlife Refuge, Ilwaco, WA 98624. 206-484-3482.

2
Oregon Coast and Coast Range

JEWELL MEADOWS WILDLIFE AREA

In Oregon's northwest corner in Clatsop County there is a damp forest, where nearly all of the timberland is owned by timber companies. (One of the small towns there is appropriately named Mist.) Roosevelt elk have always lived there, but as logging increased, bringing in more and more access roads, and the population grew, the elk and other wildlife were being crowded out.

The Oregon Department of Fish and Wildlife bought 1,200 acres in the connecting valleys where Fishhawk, Beneke, and Humbug Creeks merge, and contracted with private owners for additional buffer areas. This provides a safety zone and a place where food is always available. Among the other species using the refuge are black-tailed deer, coyotes, crows, red-tailed hawks, various songbirds, swallows, black-tailed pigeons, and an occasional bald eagle.

The annual cycle of elks' lives begins with winter feeding from the first week of December until about the first week of April. The bulls shed their antlers in March and April, and the new growth is visible a week or two later. Calves are born in May and June and the breeding season, accompanied by lots of bull bugling, runs from mid-September through mid-October.

In the immediate area is Fishhawk Creek Falls, three miles west in Lee Wooden County Park, and just east of the town of Jewell is the largest big-leaf maple in the United States. When measured in 1982, it was 34 feet 11 inches in diameter and 101 feet high with a spread of 90 feet.

The best time to visit the refuge is during the winter months, when anywhere from 75 to 200 elk can be seen almost daily from the viewpoints along State 202, which runs between Astoria and Jewell. It is a pleasant drive from Astoria along Young's Bay into the steep but low hills of the northern reaches of the Coast Range. It is a good day's outing from either Portland or the coast, taking in Saddle Mountain State Park on the same drive.

To reach Jewell Meadows, turn north off US 26 at Jewell Junction and drive on the paved but unnamed, unnumbered highway 9 miles to Jewell; turn west on State 202 and drive 1.5 miles to the refuge. There are no facilities for visitors in the area.

For more information:

Jewell Meadows Wildlife Area, Oregon Department of Fish and Wildlife, P.O. Box 59, Portland, OR 97207. 503-757-4186.

SADDLE MOUNTAIN STATE PARK

Saddle Mountain is the dominant landmark in the state's northwest corner. It can be seen from nearly all high points in Clatsop County, from the Columbia River east to the outskirts of Portland. It isn't especially tall by Cascades standards – only 3,283 feet – but that is enough to make it stand dramatically alone above the surrounding mountains.

The mountain is popular not only with hikers and picnickers but also with botanists, for it harbors several species of rare and endangered plants, some of which are not found anywhere else in the region. Consequently, it is believed that the plants predate the Ice Age and that the upper reaches of the mountain protruded above the glaciers that covered the rest of the region. Some plants are normally found only in northern regions of North America. Because the mountain has been so isolated, a few of the plants have evolved slightly to adapt to the mountain and do not fit the typical species descriptions. Most of these plants have managed to survive because they grow on rocky, mostly inaccessible parts of the mountain.

Surveys by naturalists have identified nineteen rare and

endangered plants on the mountain. Among those that grow nowhere else are the Saddle Mountain bittercress and Saddle Mountain saxifrage. The rare and endangered list includes alpine lily, pink fawn lily, hairy-stemmed sidalcea, sedge, and trillium.

Given this long list of rare and endangered plants, the state parks department pleads with hikers to stay on the 2.5-mile trail that leads from the parking lot to the summit. It winds through the evergreen forest to grassy meadows, and eventually leaves the tree line. About halfway up the mountain, the trail becomes much steeper, then traverses a series of rock ledges. Wooden bridges and platforms have been built along here for safety. The summit climb is steep so you should wear hiking boots with tread to ensure good footing.

From the summit you can see the ocean, Tillamook Head near Seaside, and much of the Cascade Range, including Mount Rainier, Mount St. Helens, Mount Adams, Mount Hood, and Mount Jefferson.

The mountain is seven miles north of US 26. The access road leaves the main highway 1.5 miles east of Necanicum Junction, or about ten miles east of Cannon Beach. The park has ten primitive tent sites and a picnic area. It is open year-round.

For more information:

Saddle Mountain State Park, 503-861-1671.

Oregon State Parks Department, 525 Trade Street S.E., Salem, OR 97310. 503-378-6305.

OREGON DUNES NATIONAL RECREATION AREA

It was late on a September afternoon when I first saw the sand dunes just south of Florence in Jesse Honeyman State Park. The sun shone in a cloudless sky; the contrast of a campground surrounded by mountainous, bone-dry dunes, with native rhododendrons so enormous they were used for screening between campsites on the shore of Cleawox Lake, and the sounds of children playing far across the lake, sliding down the dunes into the fresh water, gave me the odd feeling of being alone even though people were standing beside me.

The dunes are close to busy US 101 and its resort areas, yet they give a sense of isolation. They're a little eerie.

The Oregon dunes are among the largest in the world – up to 600 feet tall and more than a mile long – and are said to be the largest ocean-related dunes in North America. They are so high that they literally have covered a forest; occasionally the sand will shift enough to reveal the top of a tree, still standing but long dead. The dunes were formed by erosion over the centuries. Strong winds ate away at basaltic cliffs, and the ebb and flow of the surf cut away at the sandstone sea bottom. Constantly shifting, the dunes are gradually filling some of the lakes that line the coast here.

The area protected by the scenic-area designation stretches about forty miles between the Siuslaw River estuary at Florence south to Coos Bay. All along the highway are designated trails that go over the dunes toward the ocean or inland, leading to oasislike lakes with trees and rhododendrons so large that they give away the area's other secret: it may look like a desert but it is not one, because the dunes usually receive more than sixty inches of rainfall a year. Although they are rapidly filling in some of the lakes, there are naturalists who believe that within another century, vegetation will win the battle and cover the sand mountains.

Hikers enjoy the dunes and sometimes strike out across the open sand. A few things should be kept in mind, however, if you want to do the same: It is very strenuous to walk in loose sand and you will often feel that you are slipping backward as fast as you are moving forward. In addition, it is easy to become disoriented out in the dunes where you can't see anything but sand. The forest service, which administers the recreation area, urges hikers to look back occasionally so you'll recognize landmarks on your return. Don't expect to follow your own footprints – they disappear with the first breeze. You should carry a bottle of water (the freshwater lakes do not have potable water), sunglasses, a hat, sunscreen, and a light raincoat.

A good place to visit the dunes briefly if you're in a hurry is the overlook about halfway between Florence and Reedsport, where they have reached almost to the highway. You'll see signs to the overlook, which has four levels of platforms and wooden walkways, and trails leading out onto the dunes.

The dunes are a popular place for off-road-vehicle enthusiasts, but so many use the dunes that the forest service requires all vehicles, except motorcycles, to have a red flag mounted at least nine feet above ground. The heavy traffic along US 101 has created a mini-transportation industry for locals. You can go on dune-buggy rides, rent horses, or join conducted riding trips through the dunes.

For more information:

Oregon Dunes National Recreation Area, 855 Highway Avenue, Reedsport, OR 97467. 503-271-3611.

Florence Chamber of Commerce, 270 US 101, Florence OR 97439. 503-997-3128.

North Bend Information Center, 1380 Sherman, North Bend, OR 97459. 503-756-4613 or 800-824-8486.

CAPE PERPETUA

When you're driving along the Oregon Coast, you'll find that no matter how many days you have allotted for the trip, you will wish you had a few more. Places you expect to take half an hour will keep you enthralled for hours.

One such place is Cape Perpetua, three miles south of Yachats. At first glance it doesn't look any different from any of the other dozens, perhaps hundreds, of headlands that jut out into the Pacific. But Cape Perpetua has been studied long and carefully, and it has a story to tell about the geology of the coast and the people who lived there for centuries before the Europeans arrived.

The cape has been turned into a natural laboratory and classroom for the study of seasonal cycles of tide and weather, of storms, whale migrations, the relationship between sea and land, the study of plant and animal life, archaeology, and the history of timber management in the area.

The visitor center has dioramas, a popular fifteen-minute film that explains the dynamics of capes and headlands, and numerous exhibits devoted to the natural history of the area.

The cape is a basalt uprising that is composed of rock of

varying hardnesses. The sea eats away the softer rock, and this is dramatically evidenced by the narrow slit running back into the cape called the Devil's Churn. The sea thunders into this narrow gap and creates a terrific din as it reaches the end, throwing spray onto the rocks. Virtually every foot of the interpretive trails throughout the cape has something of educational value. On one exposed point you can see how the steady onshore winds have combed plants into a horizontal growth pattern, causing them almost to assume the shape of a flag in the breeze.

Archaeologists have been studying the middens (garbage dumps) along the beach left behind by the Alsi tribe that once lived in the area. The middens show what kind of shellfish they ate; in addition, deer and elk bones have been found. They also tossed various broken tools onto the garbage heap – arrow heads, clay pipes, trade beads, and articles of clothing. The Alsis also made superb canoes and watertight baskets.

Other trails lead back into the forest and up the steep mountain. One goes to a lookout built for spotting enemy aircraft and ships during World War II, and a rock lean-to built before the war by Works Progress Administration crews makes a good place to watch for whales. A two-mile driving tour goes through the forest with interpretive signs explaining the new-growth, maturing second-growth, and old-growth timber.

The forest service offers volunteers an opportunity to work on archaeological digs at the cape through the nationwide Passport in Time program. The most recent excavation is along the trail near the Devil's Churn and is open from Wednesday through Sunday each week.

For more information:

Cape Perpetua Scenic Area, P.O. Box 274, Yachats, OR 97498. 503-547-3289.

SEA LION CAVES

As discussed earlier in this book, the state of Oregon took ownership of nearly all of its coastline so the beaches could be used as a highway. When real highways were built, the coast remained in public ownership and the best sites along it were turned into state parks.

There's one exception: The Sea Lion Caves, twelve miles north of Florence, have been in private ownership since 1887. The site is one of the coast's most popular places and is reportedly the only area on the West Coast where sea lions make their home on the mainland; elsewhere, they congregate on offshore islands and rocks. The caves are the largest sea caves in North America and are among the largest in the world.

Depending on the season, the caves may be occupied by up to 600 Steller and California sea lions; other times they are almost deserted. Breeding season begins in the spring and continues through the summer. The main bulls establish harems of up to thirty cows just outside the caves, driving away younger bulls. When breeding season ends, all sea lions return to the caves for the fall and winter.

The caves were discovered by a seaman named Captain William Cox, who rowed in on a calm day, returning to them several times. According to one story, he once was stranded by a storm and had to kill a young sea lion for food. In 1887 he bought the land from the state of Oregon and his family owned it until 1926. They sold it to R. E. Clanton, who wanted to turn the caves into a tourist attraction. Clanton took on two partners, J. G. Houghton and J. E. Jacobson, and they built a 1,500-foot trail along the face of the cliff with a wooden tower down to an entrance to the caves. The attraction opened in August 1932, but there were few visitors at first because US 101 was only a gravel road then and most rivers had to be crossed by ferry. World War II halted nearly all travel along the coast, but the partners persevered and business picked up after the war ended.

The 250 stairs down to the caves proved to be too difficult for many visitors, so in 1958 the owners started construction of an elevator that would pass through 208 feet of solid rock to the caves. First a tunnel was drilled from the coastline inward to the caves, then the elevator shaft was drilled down to it. Construction work was done during the spring months when the lions were away and stopped when they returned, then resumed a year later. The elevator

DLN 93 ©

Steller sea lions at Sea Lion Caves

can carry a maximum of 23 passengers at a time and can deliver 400 persons per hour.

The caves have a floor area of about two acres and the dome rises 125 feet from the floor.

Steller sea lions are neither lions nor seals; instead, according to biologists, they are more closely related to bears. They were named for George Wilhelm Steller, the German naturalist who accompanied Vitus Bering on his second expedition to Alaska in 1741.

Steller sea lions live along the North American coast from central California all the way to the Arctic and back down the Asian coast into Japan. A recent survey by the U.S. Fish and Wildlife Service estimated the population at around 80,000, most of which can be found along the coasts of British Columbia and Alaska. The herd at Sea Lion Caves averages 200 individuals.

In addition to the sea lions, the caves support a large sea and shorebird population, including several species of gulls, cormorants, and the unusual pigeon guillemot. This bird is black with white patches and markings on its wings, and its scarlet feet trail behind when it flies, making them look like tail feathers.

Open daily, the caves are eleven miles north of Florence and thirty-eight miles south of Newport. Admission is charged and tickets are purchased in the gift shop just off the highway.

For more information:
    Sea Lion Caves, 91560 US 101, Florence, OR 97439. 503-547-3111.

OREGON COAST AQUARIUM

The Oregon Coast Aquarium opened in May 1992, and by the end of that year it was obvious that the year's-long attempt to build it was the right decision by the people of the Newport area. It was an instant success and has been praised by conservationists as well as tourism officials, who aren't always on the same side of issues.

Oregon's first major aquarium, it was created to showcase seabirds, marine mammals, fish, invertebrates, and plants. It occupies twenty-nine acres on Yaquina Bay adjacent to Oregon State University's Mark O. Hatfield Marine Science Center. Exhibits are in a 40,000-square-foot building with rock pools, caves, cliffs, and bluffs. Its exhibits replicate wetland habitats, sandy and rocky shores, and the deep ocean. Sea otters, harbor seals, sea lions, a Pacific octopus, the largest walk-through seabird aviary in North America, and tide pools are all a part of the new aquarium.

At this writing, it has 171 species represented and 6,650 or more specimens of them. Among the seabirds are tufted puffins, rhinoceros auklets, pigeon guillemots, and common murres. Harbor seals and sea lions have their own beaches and pools.

The sandy shore exhibit includes leopard sharks, flatfish, skates, sand dollars, and surfperch. In the rocky shore area you will find lampsuckers, wolf eels, sculpins, sea stars, and anemones. The coastal waters exhibit has jellyfish, basket stars, ratfish, and a variety of invertebrates, and in the wetlands exhibit are pipefish, crustaceans, and mud shrimp. The New Currents room has changing exhibits, and visitors can touch some of the sea creatures there.

The aquarium is the result of a determined group of local citizens who decided in 1981 to pursue the idea as an economic development opportunity to help relieve Newport's dependence on timber and fishing as its major sources of income. The community felt that a high-quality aquarium would increase tourism in Newport and create a demand for conferences and conventions.

The group was able to raise the $24 million it needed through contributions from federal and state agencies, foundations, corporations, and private individuals. It was established as a private, non-profit educational facility and is expected to have an annual attendance of around 750,000, of which approximately 15,000 will be school children.

It is open every day except Christmas. Hours are 9:00 A.M. to 6:00 P.M. from May 15 through October 15; 10:00 A.M. to 4:30 P.M. from October 16 through May 14. An admission fee is charged.

For more information:

Oregon Coast Aquarium, 2820 S.E. Ferry Slip Road, Newport, OR 97365. 503-867-3474.

DARLINGTONIA WAYSIDE

It looks lethal, a little like a catatonic cobra, and it *is* lethal — for the insects that are seduced by this plant, which looks good enough to eat. It is the insect that becomes lunch, though, in a macabre turn of events that enables a plant, which is usually the prey, to be the aggressor and devourer.

Commonly called pitcher plant, *Darlingtonia californica* is known as an insectivorous perennial. It is native to Oregon and northern California, but for most Oregon Coast travelers, the Darlingtonia Wayside provides the only opportunity they will have to see the plant in action.

The wayside is a sixteen-acre sphagnum bog four miles north of Florence beside US 101. One of the best times to visit is in May and June when the plants bloom. Standing as tall as three feet, each has an arched top, which resembles a hooded cobra, and a mouthlike opening. It has a strange color scheme of green with splotches of red and orange. The plants grow closely together and, to the imaginative, can appear as though they're watching you.

THE PITCHER PLANT

The entryway or "mouth" of the plant has a tonguelike appendage that secretes a sweetish fluidlike nectar, which is its irresistible bait. Once an insect is attracted inside, it gets lost because the mouth is hard to see and nearly transparent areas look like exits to it. As the insect tires from trying to get out, it slips farther and farther down the plant's slick sides. When it attempts to climb up, it encounters downward-pointing hairs which prevent it from ascending and cause it to slip deeper into the bottom of the tube, where the insect is slowly broken down by bacteria and absorbed into the plant walls as food.

The wayside has picnic tables but does not have a staff on site. You can't walk among the plants, but they are close enough to the trail that you can get good photographs of them with a long lens.

For more information:
Oregon State Parks, 525 Trade Street S.E., Salem, OR 97310. 503-378-6305.

OREGON COAST TRAIL

Ask Oregonians what the state is most proud of and nearly all will say the Oregon Coast. This is not only because the coast is so beautiful; it is mainly because in the state's early years, its leaders were wise enough to declare the beaches public property so they could be used as some of the state's first highways.

The highway department was also in charge of the state parks system, so when the highways were built along the coast, the beaches remained public and a series of state parks were established, nearly forty in all, plus numerous state-maintained waysides. Other governmental agencies opened parks, reserves, refuges, recreation areas, wildlife areas, and additional recreational sites; consequently, instead of "For Sale" or "No Trespassing" signs, the few signs that do exist tell visitors how to better enjoy the Oregon Coast.

US 101 runs the length of the coast and is a favorite route for bicyclers. Recently the Oregon Coast Trail has become popular with backpackers. While the Oregon Coast Trail lacks most of the challenges of the Pacific Crest Trail — you can drop out almost anywhere, stay in a hotel, and eat in restaurants without leaving the trail — the Oregon Coast Trail does offer a pleasant alternative to the highway route.

A word of caution: Although you won't be far from civilization, you still will be subject to the weather, which can change rapidly, chilling you to the bone in a matter of minutes. Thus, you should carry the same equipment that you would on a wilderness hike, including the famous essentials (see box below). Be prepared to carry water on long stretches of beach, and by all means make sure you have the local tidetables so you won't get stranded on the wrong side of a headland while the tide is in.

One nice thing about hiking along the coast is the great abundance of driftwood. There's so much of it that nobody cares if you have campfires; the only restriction is that you build them downwind and away from other piles of driftwood.

Some of the best and most remote hiking is along the stretches where US 101 heads inland from the coast. You will see parts of the

---

ESSENTIALS FOR HIKERS AND DAY-TRIPPERS
Water
Extra clothing and raingear
Extra food (high-energy snacks)
Sunglasses, sunscreen, and mosquito repellent
Knife
Firestarter
First-aid kit (include items for blisters and headaches)
Matches in waterproof container
Flashlight with alkaline batteries
Map
Compass
Mirror and whistle

---

coast very few people have seen, particularly on the twenty-mile section south from Bandon to Floras State Park.

The trail officially begins at the Columbia River South Jetty and ends some 360 miles later at the California border south of Brookings. It isn't complete and may never be because, by necessity, it joins US 101 or other roads where there is no other route available. This is especially true when the trail must cross a stream or go over a sheer headland, and when it goes through the Oregon dunes.

Many years ago when I worked on the Seaside *Signal*, the resort town's weekly newspaper, I hiked on Tillamook Head several times, and found it a fascinating place. It still is one of the most interesting hikes I've been on because of its historical significance — part of the Lewis and Clark expedition hiked over it from the salt-making works on Seaside's beach to Cannon Beach — and because the trail presents the best views of Tillamook Rock Lighthouse, the most forlorn of the many lighthouses built along the West Coast. About half a mile offshore, the lighthouse still stands reasonably intact in spite of being abandoned for half a century. The trail goes past the beachfront homes of Seaside, climbs up 1,200 feet to go over Tillamook Head, drops down to a point where Tillamook Rock is nicely framed by an old tree, then descends to Indian Beach, a pebbly beach with grand views of the coast. Indian Beach is also popular with surfers, who, obviously, must wear wet suits year-round. From Indian Beach the trail skirts along dramatic rocky cliffs to Ecola Point State Park, a day-use area with some of the best views of Haystack Rock and its neighbors, and of the resort town Cannon Beach.

For more information:

Coast Trail and other trails in the State Trail System (Eugene to Pacific Crest Trail, North Umpqua Trail, Forty-mile Loop Trail, and Lower Gorge Trail), Trails Coordinator, Oregon State Parks, 525 Trade Street S.E., Salem, OR 97310. 503-378-5012.

CASCADE HEAD

When the word "developer" appears in the context of environmental protection, most protectionists see red instead of green. That isn't always the most fair or accurate reaction, and Cascade Head is a good example. This small peninsula of wildness is only seven miles north of Lincoln City, one of the coast's most glitzy neon strips. The two could as easily be on opposite sides of the planet.

Cascade Head's wildness exists in part because several Oregon Coast developers anted up donations, along with hundreds of others, to enable the Nature Conservancy to purchase the headland from the farmer who had it for sale. Fortunately, he, too, wanted the land to remain unchanged, and one can only assume he didn't charge the entire market value.

The headland is one of the more moist places along this part of the coast. Rain falls on the average of every other day throughout the year, and its highlands collect up to 100 inches a year. Down on the beach rainfall measures only about seventy inches. It backs up to a dark, thick forest, which could almost be called a rain forest. Near the headland the forest gives way to open hills with a carpet of wildflowers mixed among the salal and low-growing spruces, Indian paintbrushes, asters, mosses, and berries. The headland is also one

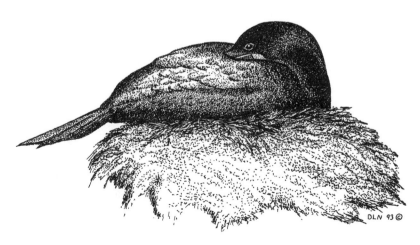

A cormorant nests along the Oregon coast

of only three places worldwide that supports the threatened Oregon silverspot butterfly, which is a mottled orange and brown.

Several trails lace Cascade Head, but by far the most popular is the two-mile (each way) Nature Conservancy path that goes through the lush forest and out on the meadows, where it is too windy for trees to grow. The trail gives you some of the most sweeping views along the coast, and the interplay of the ocean, coastline, and weather is never boring to watch from a vantage point like this. Fences have been built to protect delicate plants along the edge of the headlands and to keep people from disturbing sea life below.

Some whale-watchers come to the head to watch the migration of the grays from December through May, although the best one can hope for is simply a glimpse of the spouts.

To reach the trailhead, turn off US 101 seven miles north of Lincoln City onto Forest Service Road 1861 and follow it between two and three miles to the Nature Conservancy trailhead.

For more information:

Siuslaw National Forest, 4077 S.W. Research Way, Corvallis, OR 97333. 503-757-4480.

Nature Conservancy, 1234 N.W. 25th, Portland, OR 97210. 503-228-9561.

OREGON ISLANDS NATIONAL WILDLIFE REFUGE

About 1,500 islands, ranging from sharp boulders protruding above high tide to pieces of land large enough for buildings, line the Oregon Coast from Cannon Beach south to Brookings. These islands, totaling only about 575 acres, are a major component of the coast's beauty; they are used as backdrops for sunset photos and add variety to the views from beach homes and hotels.

They also provide places for birds and sea mammals to nest and rest away from people and predators. As such, most have been designated wildernesses and national wildlife refuges. Consequently, they are at once the nearest but most inaccessible wilderness areas and wildlife refuges in the state. Some are close enough to the shore to wade out to at low tide, but the laws do not allow this, nor can you take a boat closer than 200 yards to them.

Only two offshore islands have ever supported humans: Tillamook Rock and Zwagg Island. Tillamook Rock is the farthest north of the islands, about a half mile off Tillamook Head between Seaside and Cannon Beach. A lighthouse was built on Tillamook Rock and put into service in 1879. To be stationed there was almost like being sentenced to a two- or three-person Alcatraz because it was so difficult to get on and off. The lighthouse, which was finally closed in 1957 and replaced by an automated light on shore, has most recently been used as a mausoleum. Zwagg Island, offshore from Brookings, was named (but misspelled) for a Dutch hermit named Folker Von Der Zwaag, who lived on the island in the 1890s.

Throughout the spring and summer – April through August – the comic-looking puffins, the less colorful but more energetic murres, and the auklets and murrelets cover much of the rocks with their nests. When they leave, the next group of residents – grebes, loons, and scoters – replace them, while the more permanent residents – gulls and cormorants – ignore the comings and goings of their migratory relatives.

Comic-looking puffins

Among the sea mammals found here are harbor seals and sea lions. During the spring you can often see gray whales migrating slowly northward from the Sea of Cortez to the waters off Alaska.

For more information:
Western Oregon National Wildlife Refuge Complex, 26208 Finley Refuge Road, Corvallis, OR 97333. 503-757-7236.

ROGUE RIVER NATIONAL SCENIC WATERWAY

The Rogue River comes crashing down through the Coast Range, creating Oregon's most popular white-water runs and providing some of the best fishing on the West Coast. The river has been a favorite of many famous fishermen, including Zane Gray, Jack London, Gary Cooper, and Clark Gable. President Herbert Hoover, after being criticized for fishing on the Rogue River when he could have been tending the nation's ills, supposedly uttered one of the most famous statements about the value of fishing: "The hours a man spends fishing do not count against his total life span."

Wilderness lovers and white-water enthusiasts appreciate the Rogue as much as fishermen. The more adventurous go back into the mountains from the Grants Pass area or upriver from Gold Beach and Wederburn to ride kayaks and inflatables over the wild rapids. Along the road that now follows the river all the way to the sea, you

---

WHITE-WATER RATINGS

Class 1 - Easy
Class 2 - Moderate
Class 3 - Dangerous. Novices should consider lining or portaging boats.
Class 4 - Very dangerous. Novices should line or portage.
Class 5 - Extremely dangerous. Even experts should consider portaging.
Class 6 - Unrunnable. Portage boats.

---

will find outfitters to take you on float or fishing trips. Down at Gold Beach and Wederburn you can ride on swift jetboats that go upriver to Agness, duplicating the popular mailboat run of years past when no roads penetrated the wilderness.

For the less adventurous, the drive through the mountains from US 101 to I-5 is one of the more beautiful mountain routes in Oregon. It is best to allow a full day for the trip, not because of the distance as much as to allow for slow driving where the road is unpaved and for frequent stops to enjoy particularly pretty spots.

Backpackers like the forty-mile trek between Illahe on the western side upstream to Grave Creek. The trail follows the river-bank in some places but long stretches of it are high above the river along shelves too narrow for horses, which means backpackers can trudge along without always having to watch where they step. Several viewpoints along the way provide good opportunities to photograph kayaks and inflatables tumbling through the rapids.

The trail can be divided into smaller, more manageable portions, and the jetboats that run on a daily schedule can be used for transportation in and out, avoiding the problem of spotting a car or van at either end of the hike. If you plan to take your own kayak or inflatable down the Rogue, be aware that the river can be used only by permit. In an average year, the forest service issues 10,000 permits; however, up to 100,000 requests are made annually, so the lottery system is used to determine who gets the permits. Consequently, it is simpler to go with a commercial guide.

For more information:

Siskiyou National Forest, 200 N.E. Greenfield Road, Grants Pass, OR 97526. 503-479-5301.

Rogue River National Forest, 333 West 8th Street, Medford, OR 97501. 503-776-3600.

3
Willamette Valley

METRO WASHINGTON PARK ZOO

One of the more refreshing changes in zoos lately is the switch from capturing wild animals and putting them in zoos for people to stare at. Although I am not an animal-rights activist by any definition, this aspect of zoos always bothered me and I refused to take my children to them when they were young. Now I would gladly take my grandchildren to zoos that perform a more useful function, such as trying to preserve endangered species.

Portland's Metro Washington Park Zoo does exactly that. It is active in ten Species Survival Plans (SSP), which means it works with other zoos in a worldwide breeding plan to preserve vanishing species. Of thirty-seven endangered species under protection by the program, the zoo is involved with the Asian elephant, snow leopard, Siberian tiger, orangutan, red panda, spectacled bear, chimpanzee, red-ruffed lemur, black rhino, and Humboldt penguin. It has the most successful breeding program for Asian elephants in the world; twenty-five have been born since 1962. The herd now consists of three males, seven females, and two juveniles.

The Africa Rain Forest exhibit combines West African art, culture, plants, and animals, including fruit bats, striped mongoose, a rock python, L'Hoests monkeys, Cape clawless otters, and numerous tropical African birds.

The Africa exhibit shows the dry, open bush country of East Africa and has black rhinos, Nile hippos, Hartmann's mountain zebras, impalas, DeBrazza's monkeys, and other East African animals.

DLN 93 ©

A beaver in the zoo's western Cascades exhibit

The Penguinarium houses twenty-five endangered Humboldt penguins and a flock of Inca terns. The Alaska Tundra exhibit has animals of the region in a replicated tundra ecosystem. The Cascade Exhibit is a representation of the plant and animal life of the western Cascades, including beavers, otters, dippers, fish, reptiles, amphibians, and waterfowl.

The zoo opens daily at 9:30 A.M. and offers a train ride through its sixty-one acres. An admission fee is charged.

OREGON'S BATS

Fifteen species of bats live in Oregon. All feed on insects, including pests such as spruce budworm moths, tussock moths, mosquitoes, pine bark beetle moths, and gypsy moths. The forest service estimates it would have to spend $26 million a year to combat these pests if bats disappeared form Oregon's forests.

For more information:

Metro Washington Park Zoo, 4001 S.W. Canyon Road, Portland, OR 97221. 503-226-1561.

NATIONAL WILDLIFE REFUGES OF THE WILLAMETTE VALLEY

For countless centuries the entire population of the dusky Canada goose has migrated south from the Copper River delta in Alaska and wintered in the Willamette Valley. With the arrival of farming in the middle of the last century and the steady decline in suitable habitat, this unique species began declining toward extinction. So in the

A merganser at William Finley Wildlife Refuge

1960s the Fish and Wildlife Service began buying up land along the Willamette River in the Salem-Corvallis area and created three refuges especially for the geese: Baskett Slough, Ankeny, and William Finley National Wildlife Refuges.

Each of the refuges has agreements on a share basis with local farmers to grow crops such as ryegrass, fescue grass, sudan grass, cereal grains, and corn. Dikes and ponds also have been built to attract the waterfowl.

Basket Slough covers 2,492 acres of farmland on an ancient lake bed surrounded by rolling hills with oak timber on them. Named for an early resident, George J. Baskett, the refuge includes Morgan Lake and is home for several varieties of waterfowl in addition to songbirds and a variety of mammals. A total of almost 200 species of wildlife have been counted on the refuge.

To reach it, drive twelve miles west of Salem on State 22 to State 99W, then continue west on State 22 for 12.5 miles.

The Ankeny refuge is 2,796 acres of rich bottomland just northeast of the confluence of the Willamette and Santiam rivers. Named for an early dairy farmer in the area, Ankeny has several cleared farm fields crisscrossed by ditches and hedgerows of berry briars, roses, hawthornes, and ash, which provide cover for the wildlife.

To go there, turn west off I-5 at the Talbot exit, which is ten miles north of Albany, then head north on Jorgenson Road and west on Wintel Road.

William Finley National Wildlife Refuge has 5,325 acres with a similar mix of farmland, wooded hills, and wetlands. It was named for an early naturalist who is credited with persuading President Theodore Roosevelt to create the first national wildlife refuges. In addition to the dusky Canada geese, the Finley refuge hosts wood ducks and hooded mergansers during the summer months, and also ruffed grouse, ring-necked pheasants, California and mountain quail, doves, and black-tailed deer. This is the only one of the three refuges to have a self-guided trail, which is open the year-round.

To visit the refuge, drive eleven miles south of Corvallis on State 99W to the entrance road, which is on the west side of the highway.

All refuges have areas that are open to the public the year-round, but as with most, some parts will be closed all the time and others will be closed during critical periods, such as hatching time.

For more information:

Western Oregon Refuges, Refuge Manager, 26208 Finley Refuge Road, Corvallis, OR 97333. 503-757-7236.

SILVER FALLS STATE PARK

There's something about waterfalls . . .

Some deep thinkers who believe all life came from the sea feel that part of the great attraction of the seacoast is a primal urge to return to our birthplace. But what about the appeal of waterfalls? Is this a part of the same attraction or does it have something to do with flying? Perhaps it is no more complicated than our innate love for natural beauty since few things in nature are more beautiful than moving water — nature's circulatory system — whether it be from rain or snow working its way back to sea or man-made fountains. Whatever the root of the attraction, few things in the human experience are more soothing than water in motion.

Silver Falls State Park is probably the best place to go in Oregon to watch falling water. None of the fourteen named waterfalls here is as high as Multnomah Falls in the Columbia Gorge, but size isn't the only criterion for beauty. The falls in this park range in height from only a few feet to 178 feet.

The falls occur in a cluster of small V-shaped canyons twenty-six miles east of Salem on State 214. After you see them it will be no surprise that the state park is one of the most popular in Oregon. It has more than 100 campsites — 53 with electrical hookups and 51 tent sites — picnic shelters, lodging for groups, a fourteen-mile equestrian trail, a horse camp, a three-mile jogging trail, and a four-mile bike trail. In spite of this, the park retains its wilderness feeling because at nearly 9,000 acres it is the largest in Oregon. Also, the seven-mile hiking trail to the falls is like all trails that long; after one or two miles, the traffic thins and by the time you reach the last waterfall you will have very little competition for viewpoints.

The most popular trail, called the "Trail of Ten Falls," takes you near or behind ten falls ranging from 27 to 178 feet high. Another trail goes five miles to Lower South Falls and on to Lower North, Double, Drake, and Middle North falls. Other trails include a four-mile biking trail, fourteen miles of equestrian trails, and a three-mile jogging trail.

The waterfalls were formed when the lava that covered the area was broken and tilted upward at the time the Cascade Range was formed. Silver Creek resulted from the Cascade uplift and cut its way through the basalt on its way downward.

The park has a conference center with lodges that have six bedrooms each, a public dining hall, and meeting rooms. Large groups, such as family reunions and company gatherings, are held in two centers called the Ranches. The park also has a youth camp, a group camp with tent sites, a horse camp with primitive camping and corrals, and an overnight campground with 104 sites, plus hot showers and restrooms.

For more information:

Silver Falls State Park, 503-873-8681.

Oregon State Parks Campsite Information Center, 800-452-5687 in Oregon; 503-238-7488 in Portland and out of Oregon.

State Park Regional Office, 3554 S.E. 82nd Avenue, Portland, OR 97266. 503-731-3293.

4
Cascade Range

PACIFIC CREST TRAIL

Is there a backpacker in the world who hasn't vowed to hike the Pacific Crest Trail, or at least part of it? For several years I talked about hiking the section in Washington between Stevens and Snoqualmie Passes with my son and one of his friends, but never did. Like hiking the Appalachian Trail, kayaking from Paris to the Mediterranean, or traversing the Sahara with camel drovers, hiking the Pacific Crest Trail remains one of those unfulfilled dreams for most people.

Failing to hike it isn't something to wring your hands over in your dotage because it is a long, hard trip: 2,600 miles from Canada to Mexico over mountains of all heights and types, through swamps and deserts. Its elevation ranges from a high of 13,200 feet near

---

TRAIL TERMINOLOGY
The forest service offers these three categories of hiking trails:

EASY: Free of obstacles, grades of 10 percent or less, with safe and well-marked trails.

MODERATE: May have roots and embedded rocks on the trail and sustained grades up to 20 percent.

DIFFICULT: Roots, embedded rocks, and other obstacles and sustained grades up to 30 percent.

TIME/DISTANCE: As a general rule, allow thirty minutes for each mile hiked.

Mount Whitney in California to near sea level in the Columbia Gorge. The average elevations in each state are 6,000 in California, 5,000 in Oregon, and 4,000 in Washington.

In Oregon, it comes up from California south of Ashland and crosses I-5, then heads north toward Crater Lake, bisects the Diamond Peak Wilderness, Three Sisters Wilderness, Mount Jefferson Wilderness, and goes around Mount Hood before dropping down to the Columbia River. Its route takes it across seven or eight cross-Cascades highways, which makes it easy to hike it in the segments between highways.

Although several people have hiked the whole route – a few in one outing rather than section by section over a period of years – for the purposes of this book we will look only at the Oregon portion, which covers about 425 miles, and will concentrate on one of the more accessible portions for those who would like to try it.

The trail has been worked on almost constantly over the last several years and the changes are definitely for the better, because at one time parts of it were marked by blazed trees or by plastic strips attached to bushes or trees. For some sections the trail could be seen only because someone had been there before, leaving behind footprints. Now most of it is broad and well tended, with footbridges over many of the streams. These improvements have by no means turned it into a boulevard, nor eliminated the steepness, but they have made it easier on your good nature and boots.

A fifty-five-mile stretch that is convenient and popular with many hikers is in the shadow of Mount Hood from State 35 near Barlow Pass to the Columbia River. It is easy to arrange rides from both ends and the scenery is spectacular. You hike through a wide variety of terrains and can stop at Timberline Lodge, one of Oregon's most famous landmarks.

To begin on the southern end, drive east on US 26 and turn north on State 35 near the summit of the Cascades. The trail begins near the Barlow Pass summit and follows the Skyline Trail some of the time. (The Skyline is part of an earlier trail system that goes around Mount Hood.)

The trail traverses ancient Mount Hood mudflows and hillsides of exposed sediments washed down from the loose soil of the mountain. After a bit more than three miles the trail leads you into the parking lot of Timberline Lodge, one of the most magnificent of the lodges built during the Works Progress Administration in the 1930s. From there, the trail stays above timberline most of the time as it goes around the western side of Mount Hood, fording several glacial streams and passing glacial deposits of sand and gravel, then descends into the viewless — and mostly windless — Mount Hood National Forest. The noise level increases when you reach streams that almost inevitably take you past waterfalls. This keeps the trail from being a straight-line march for it must make several jogs in search of good places to ford streams.

The last part of the hike is the best because of the descent into the Columbia Gorge. It offers you two choices of routes: to follow the main Pacific Crest Trail or to take the alternate Eagle Creek Trail, which is about the same length but goes through a more scenic area. Eagle Creek should win, hands down. It is strenuous, particularly the descent into the Columbia Gorge, and a little scary for anyone prone to acrophobia. But this is one of the prettiest parts of the hike, especially when Eagle Creek becomes a series of waterfalls that finally end in Eagle Creek Gorge near Cascade Locks, one of the Columbia Gorge's most beautiful side trips.

For more information:

Mount Hood National Forest, 2955 N.W. Division, Gresham, OR 97030. 503-666-0700.

MOUNT HOOD WILDERNESS

This mountain, which forms such a perfect backdrop for Portland, is still an active volcano and undoubtedly will one day erupt again. It has had several "incidents" since the arrival of Europeans, including eruptions of steam and ash in the 1800s, and in 1907 it got so hot that part of White River Glacier melted and created floods.

Most of the 11,237-foot mountain and its surroundings are protected by the Mount Hood Wilderness. The southern slopes remain open to development because of the ski areas and the magnificent Timberline Lodge that sits at the 6,000-foot level.

Timberline Lodge is one of Oregon's most treasured destinations. A National Historic Site, it is one of the largest wooden buildings ever built and is said to be the only twentieth-century building of its size built and furnished entirely by hand. It is a tribute to the legacy of President Franklin Roosevelt's Works Progress Administration, which sponsored its construction, and gathered decorations of local artwork and crafts, including hand-loomed draperies of wool and flax grown in Oregon.

Timberline is equally well-known for snow sports; some of Oregon's best downhill skiing is on the southern slopes, and cross-country skiing is popular all around the mountain. It has five downhill ski areas, four of which offer night skiing. It also has three

DLN 93 ©

Mount Hood

groomed areas for nordic skiing plus nearly 200 kilometers of un-groomed trails.

The next most popular sport is climbing; some 10,000 persons climb Mount Hood each year because it is one of the easiest major American peaks to climb. Women in heels and a man with no legs have reached the summit. One runner left Timberline Lodge and arrived at the summit one hour and twenty-five minutes later.

However, this has also created a multitude of problems for search-and-rescue organizations and Mount Hood has one of the worst safety records of any major American peak. Many people have died because it can be as treacherous as Denali or Mount Rainier. Always have the proper equipment—crampons, ice axe, rope, helmet, and a respectful attitude—especially on those hot summer days when you can't believe it is possible to get chilly.

Hiking and backpacking are the most popular forms of recreation around the mountain, and the Mount Hood Wilderness has numerous trails for that purpose. The most heavily used is the thirty-eight-mile Timberline Trail, which goes all the way around the mountain. This trip takes three to five days and usually begins and ends at the Timberline Lodge—a great place to end a hike. Another two dozen or more trails lead into the wilderness. Some are circular while other routes dead-end at glaciers or other natural barriers.

For more information:

Mount Hood National Forest, 2955 N.W. Division Street, Gresham, OR 97030. 503-677-0511.

Timberline Lodge, Timberline, OR 97028. 503-231-7979 or 800-452-1335.

BULL OF THE WOODS WILDERNESS AREA

This wilderness, tucked away high in the Cascades between Mount Hood and Mount Jefferson, is one of the most remote of the state's wilderness areas. It is partly for this reason that it has one of the last old-growth reserves of western hemlock, yellow cedar, and Douglas fir remaining in Oregon.

The wilderness area isn't especially large, so it is attractive to those who like their hikes leisurely and limited to only a few miles. The most popular day hike is from the trailhead off State 224 from Estacada, then 1.5 miles to Bagby Hot Springs. The trail leads through towering old-growth to rock-rimmed pools. A ranger is in residence to enforce no camping bans in the area.

Another easy hike is just over a mile long to Pansy Lake, where swimming is permitted. The trail to the top of Bull of the Woods peak, where a lookout tower stands, is not quite so easy but rewarding for its views. It is staffed during the fire season and serves as an emergency shelter. From the peak and lookout you will be able

The rare northern spotted owl

to see the line of peaks of the Cascades as far north as Mount Rainier and south to Three Sisters.

Since the area is so remote, you usually won't be bothered by many other people, which makes it popular with bird-watchers. It is notable for the number and species of owls living among the old-growth, including the bellwether of logging restrictions, the northern spotted owl. Other owls include the great horned owl, the screech owl, the pygmy owl, the saw-whet owl, and the flammulated owl.

For more information:

Mount Hood National Forest, 2955 N.W. Division Street, Gresham, OR 97030. 503-667-0511.

Willamette National Forest, P.O. Box 907, Baker, OR 97814. 503-523-6391.

LITTLE NORTH SANTIAM RIVER HIKE

This river valley, just south of Bull of the Woods Wilderness Area, has long been a battleground between preservationists and loggers because of its groves of ancient Douglas fir and western hemlock. After traveling along the river by car and on foot, it is easy to see why the preservationists have been working so hard.

The prettiest part of the valley is Opal Creek Grove, a 32,320-acre tract, which has the emerald Opal Pool as its centerpiece. This pool is near the mouth of Opal Creek where it enters the Little North Fork Santiam River. The rest of the creek is as beautiful, with delicate vine maple leaves framed by the dark forest, an occasional Pacific yew tree (source of the cancer drug taxol), berries, and ferns.

The Little North Santiam trail begins at a gate on Forest Service Road 2209 (see directions below) and goes past noisy waterfalls and forests so silent a bird's song comes as a surprise. The hike can be made throughout the year because snowfall is seldom a problem.

The Opal Creek Trail swings off the main trail and is fairly new at this writing. A bit less than two miles long, its length will double with the completion of a footbridge, handrails, and additional trail built by the forest service and volunteers. The trail's existence is due largely to the generosity of the Shiny Rock Mining Corporation, which once mined silver and zinc in the area. After it shut down its operation, the company gave its facilities at a place called Jawbone Flat to the Friends of Opal Creek. The organization will conduct research and educational projects related to the forest.

To reach the trailhead, drive east from Salem on State 22 to Mehama and turn left on Little North Fork Road. After about sixteen miles it becomes Forest Road 2209. Follow it another four miles past the intersection with Forest Road 2207 and park at the gate.

For more information:

Willamette National Forest, 211 East Seventh Avenue, Eugene, OR 97440. 503-465-6521.

Detroit Ranger Station, HC73, Box 320, Mill City, OR 97360. 503-854-3366.

Friends of Opal Creek, 503-897-2921.

Guided trips are led by Ancient Forest Adventures, 16 N.W. Kansas Avenue, Bend, OR 97701-1202. 503-385-8633 or 800-551-1043.

FALL CREEK TRAIL

This trail, conveniently broken into five segments for those who have the time or interest in only a day hike, goes through both new- and old-growth forest. It has been designated a National Recreation Trail, in part because of the series of trailheads along its thirteen miles, plus campgrounds, picnic areas, and short nature trails.

The western, downstream section has old-growth Douglas fir and western hemlock towering over alder as well as big-leaf and vine maple trees. The upstream end is through both old- and second-growth timber. The trail gains only about 400 feet in its thirteen miles, from about 1,000 to 1,400 feet. There seldom is snow at this low elevation, so the trail can be hiked with comfort nearly year-round.

Fall Creek is a particularly beautiful stream, and the trail keeps it in sight most of the route. It has waterfalls, riffles, quiet and dark pools, and dramatic rock formations hanging over it.

Overnight hikers have a choice of three campgrounds: Dolly Varden, Bedrock, and Puma. Day visitors can hike a segment of the trail, fish, picnic, or go for a short walk on the nature trail at Johnny Creek Campground.

The trail is reached by driving east of Eugene on State 58 to Lowell. From the Lowell Ranger Station, drive two miles on the Jasper Lowell Road, turn right at the Unity covered bridge, and follow that road, which becomes Forest Road 18, for about ten miles to the first trailhead, which is across Fall Creek from Dolly Varden Campground. Other trailheads are scattered along the way upstream, all on the opposite side of the river from the trail.

For more information:

Willamette National Forest, 211 East Seventh Avenue, Eugene, OR 97440. 503-465-6521.

Lowell Ranger Station, Lowell, OR 97452. 503-937-2129.

THREE SISTERS WILDERNESS

This wilderness area is not only one of Oregon's largest but also one of its most heavily used. This is partly because it is so beautiful and encompasses many lakes and mountains with an abundance of hiking trails. Another reason is that Bend and Sunriver, two of Oregon's fastest-growing cities, are only a short distance east of the wilderness boundaries. Mount Butte, the most popular downhill ski area in the state, is also on the eastern edge of the wilderness along State 46, called Century Drive, which forms much of the northeastern boundary.

It gets its name from three distinctive and related peaks with the geographically descriptive, if unimaginative, names of North Sister, Middle Sister, and South Sister. All are just over 10,000 feet (10,085, 10,047, and 10,358, respectively) and present one of Oregon's most beautiful mountain profiles. A fourth peak, Broken Top, completes the area's profile. It is south of the Sisters and stands 9,175 feet. Some geologists originally believed this group of peaks was part of a single volcano that had blown itself to smithereens, and they named it Mount Multnomah. Researchers eventually found that the three peaks were three separate volcanoes.

The wilderness is one of Oregon's most popular destinations for hikers. The Pacific Crest Trail traverses it and each road leading to its boundaries from all sides has numerous trailheads. The most heavily used trails and campgrounds are along State 46. One of the most popular leads four miles into the wilderness from Sparks Lake to the foot of South Sister's Green Lakes Basin.

South Sister is one of the easiest to climb and requires no special technical skills, although like any strenuous activity, good physical condition is essential. The route is 5.6 miles and the elevation gain is gradual.

North Sister is said to be the most difficult of the group because of extremely loose scree and snow. Middle Sister requires no special technical skills nor does Broken Top.

With this said, you should be aware that the mountains have a history of numerous calls for mountain-rescue teams. Most are related to weather because it is so changeable along the Cascades. Also, too many hikers and climbers do not take the proper equipment.

This part of the Cascade Range is famous for its powder snow so alpine skiing is another popular activity in the wilderness, especially off the loop highway, State 46, which is regularly plowed for the convenience of downhillers at Mount Bachelor. Several good cross-country ski trails lead off this highway, and many of the trails are marked.

For more information:

On the eastern side of the wilderness, contact Deschutes National Forest, 1645 US 20 East, Bend, OR 97701. 503-388-2715.

Much of the western side is managed by Willamette National Forest, 211 East Seventh Avenue, Eugene, OR 97440. 503-465-6522.

5
Blue Mountains

HELLS CANYON NATIONAL RECREATION AREA

Six thousand feet deep and up to ten miles wide from rim to rim, Hells Canyon is the deepest canyon in North America – if not the whole world – and one of the most remote places in the Northwest. The Snake River thunders through the canyon, forming the boundary between Oregon and Idaho. It drops more than eleven feet per mile as it plunges over riffles and rapids before flattening as it reaches the Idaho-Washington border.

This national recreation area was created on December 31, 1975, after a long struggle by its proponents to keep various agencies from damming it up. It happened with little time to spare because two dams – Hells Canyon and Oxbow Dam – were already in place on the southern end of what became the recreation area. The national recreation area designation ensured that the Snake River would remain wild and free through the canyon, and that 652,488 acres of the canyon and its rim would remain untouched. The designation makes no attempt to remove all motorized vehicles from the canyon, as a wilderness designation would, because powerboats have shot up and down the canyon for decades, and still do: That buzzing you may hear is not a horsefly.

If it is silence and roadless country you want, bear in mind that the recreation area consists largely of Hells Canyon Wilderness, which covers most of the Oregon side of the river and the part of the Idaho side that is roadless. The remainder of the NRA is a broad buffer zone that protects the wilderness lands. Still more protection was given the river itself when a 31.5-mile section from Hells

Pausing above Hells Canyon

Canyon Dam downriver to Oittsburg Landing won a Wild and Scenic River designation.

All of this means the area remains mostly roadless. You can approach the canyon from the south from the town of Halfway. The road crosses the Snake River into Idaho just downstream of the Oxbow Dam and follows the river down to Hells Canyon Dam. Otherwise, to get into the canyon, you must go by boat, horseback, or foot. Any of these three methods requires endurance and skill.

If you want to use a boat, do some careful research first because the large, swift river is filled with rapids; once you are on it you are committed to the entire canyon — there are no takeout places for miles. During the summer months you must obtain a permit to launch a boat in the river. Unless you have a lot of experience in whitewater and wilderness travel, you will be better off going with an outfitter who specializes in this.

If you are going by horseback or hiking, be aware that although several trails totaling about 1,000 miles are shown on maps, some are well maintained but many are not and therefore are very difficult for horses and hikers. To repeat, you will probably have a better trip if you work with a licensed outfitter in the area.

One trail of particular interest is the Nee-Me-Poo Trail on the northern end of the NRA. It is part of the route taken by the Nez Perce during their famous flight from the Wallowa Valley. The chief was able to get his people across the river at flood stage without losing anyone, but the U.S. Army was afraid to follow them for their horses were weighed down with heavy equipment. This 3.7-mile route has been designated a National Historic Trail.

Three trails have been designated National Recreation Trails: the Western Rim Trail, which is thirty-seven miles long; the Heavens Gate Trail, which is only one-sixth of a mile long and goes to a lookout tower; and the Snake River Trail, which runs forty-eight miles along the Idaho rim.

About twenty campgrounds have been established in the NRA, and boaters and backpackers can camp along the river and trails. Be aware that the area is quite arid and you will have to carry a generous supply of water, especially during the dry summer months. All water you take from streams and ponds or lakes must, *without exception*, be treated before drinking or cooking.

Two things to keep you on your toes are rattlesnakes, which are common in the canyon, and poison ivy, which grows in abundance on the lower elevations. If you see a shiny three-leaved plant with white berries, do not touch. Ticks are still another pest to watch

---

THE BEASTS

Oregon has very few dangerous critters. Only occasionally will you encounter a rattlesnake—most outdoorsmen go for years without seeing one. Oregon has some black bears, which present no danger except, perhaps, to your food supply if you don't hang it from a tree branch at night. The most dangerous beast in the whole state is *Giardia*, the microscopic organism that causes the stomach disorder known as "beaver fever." It is the reason you must purify all drinking water by boiling it for ten minutes, using chemicals, or using approved filtration devices.

RUFFLING FEATHERS
Snipe are famous for their courtship flights on the breeding grounds. During these flights, a rapid-dive display produces an eerie wailing sound as the wind whistles through the birds' vibrating tail feathers. The sound can be mistaken for an owl and is known as "winnowing."

---

out for and you should check your body for them daily because they can spread Rocky Mountain spotted fever.

Because the canyon is so deep, it encompasses a variety of microclimates from the rim down to the river. As you travel at different levels you can expect to see at least a few of the 350 or more species of wildlife that have been recorded in this area. During the spring you will probably see Canada geese, merganser ducks, the blue lazuli bunting, various warblers, deer, elk, bighorn sheep, tree frogs, four or five kinds of owls, river otters, snipes, badgers, various kinds of raptors – including golden eagles – and occasionally a bobcat. The river is home to the giant white sturgeon, which can grow up to twelve feet long, but don't expect to see the migratory fish such as salmon and steelhead; the hydroelectric dams killed off their runs.

For more information:

Hells Canyon National Recreation Area Headquarters, P.O. Box 490, Enterprise, OR 97828. 503-426-4978.

Hells Canyon National Recreation Area, P.O. Box 699, Clarkston, WA 99403. 509-758-0616. For river reservations and information, 509-758-1957, or 208-743-2297 in the Riggins, Idaho, office.

Wallowa-Whitman National Forest Headquarters, P.O. Box 907, Baker City, OR 97814. 503-523-6391.

EAGLE CAP WILDERNESS

This is one of Oregon's most remote wilderness areas, tucked far over in the northeast corner of the state in the Wallowa Mountains and not really on the way to anywhere else. Only in recent years has the road been opened to north-south through traffic from the Washington border to the southern end of Hells Canyon. Before this most traffic stopped at Wallowa Lake, and some continued east to the edge of the Hells Canyon at Imnaha, but the roads were poor.

Most of the 358,461 acres of Eagle Cap Wilderness remains isolated. A few areas are heavily used, particularly where saddle horses are permitted, but if you select trails that are off-limits to horses, you will be able to spend a lot of time alone with your companions and your own thoughts.

Eagle Cap has an abundance of high alpine lakes, meadows that are filled with flowers during the alpine spring in June and July, several U-shaped valleys carved by glaciers centuries ago, lots of timber, and many rock faces that provide great views across the wilderness. Among the wildlife you can expect to see are mountain goats, bighorn sheep, deer, elk, ground squirrels, picas, and other smaller mammals.

The wilderness takes in much of the Wallowa Mountains, which are part of the Blue Mountains and among the most beautiful in Oregon. They surround the lush and picturesque valley where the towns of Enterprise and Joseph were built, and where the picture-perfect Wallowa Lake stands at the edge of the mountains. Wallowa Lake State Park is one of Oregon's most popular, so reservations for campsites are often difficult to come by, for families book them far in advance.

Across the road from Wallowa Lake State Park you can enter Eagle Cap Wilderness in a most unusual manner: from a commercially operated gondola. The Mount Howard Gondola owners say it is the longest and steepest gondola ride in North America. It goes from the lake level, where the elevation is about 3,200 feet, to the snack bar and gift shop at the landing 3,500 feet higher. When you step off the gondola, you will feel as though you've gone from one country to another because you will be in an alpine zone above the timberline, and to say the views are panoramic is to practice understatement. You can see the glacial moraines around Wallowa Lake, the ranches and wheat farms up valley that look like pieces of jigsaw puzzles, the Blue Mountains along the Oregon-Washington border, the mountains of the Hells Canyon National Recreation Area, and on into Idaho.

The circular hike is twelve miles from Mount Howard to Aneroid Lake and back down to Wallowa Lake. There is no established trail for the first part of the hike, just the open ridge top to follow south from the gondola until you see Aneroid Lake ahead and below. The danger of getting lost is minimal as long as you keep the lake in sight, so some hikers branch off and climb one or two of the nearby peaks, all over 9,000 feet, for more exercise and to enjoy the views.

Several good campsites are scattered around Aneroid Lake and the nearby, smaller Roger Lake. The way back to Wallowa Lake is on Trail No. 1804, nearly all of it downhill. The first two miles aren't particularly steep but the final four are, so be sure you've made that most necessary preparation for the hike: clipped toenails.

Some hearty hikers complete the trip in a single day after catching the first gondola car at 10:00 A.M. but most prefer to extend the trip so it lasts at least two days.

The wilderness is also a popular winter sports area. Local outdoorsmen have formed the Eagle Cap Nordic Ski Club, which has a winter camp near Big Sheep Creek. The camp has a 12-by-14-foot wall tent with bunks for six people, a woodstove, firewood, lantern, and small cache of food. It is available for use by anyone in the area, but reservations are needed. Check with the forest service for details.

For more information:

Wallowa-Whitman National Forest, P.O. Box 907, Baker, OR 97814. 503-523-6391.

Wallowa Valley Ranger District, Route 1, Box M, Enterprise, OR 97846. 503-432-2171.

Eagle Cap Ranger District, P.O. Box M, Joseph, OR 97828. 503-426-3104.

Joseph Chamber of Commerce, 102 East First, Joseph, OR 97846. 503-432-1015.

Wallowa County Chamber of Commerce, 88401 State 82, Enterprise, OR 97828. 503-426-4978.

JOSEPH CANYON

One of Oregon's most famous citizens was a Nez Perce chief named Joseph, who was the wise leader of a small band that lived in the Wallowa Valley. There were two Josephs who led the band in peacetime activities, as opposed to the warrior chiefs. The elder Joseph had been a diplomatic leader and managed to get along with the people who began moving into his valley. When he died and his son took over, it was rare that the son was as wise and humane as the father.

Gradually relations between the Native Americans and the newcomers grew strained and finally broke down entirely in 1877 when a white man shot a Nez Perce for questionable reasons. Thus the war began; the army was called in to put down the uprising and to move Chief Joseph's band to a reservation. Joseph and his people had no choice but to flee their beloved Wallowa Valley. He had only a few warriors but many elderly people, women, and children. Some were ill and others quickly became ill.

Joseph's plan was simple: To get out of the United States and into Canada where the Nez Perce had friends and relatives. Joseph led this slow-moving group on a trek in the middle of winter, heading north and across the Snake River into Idaho and Montana, foraging as they went, always outsmarting the army in spite of its fresh horses and well-fed men. But his people were getting weaker and weaker, some were dying, and Joseph could no longer stand to see them suffer so. They were almost within sight of Canada when he had to admit defeat and surrender. He told the army that from where the sun stood at that moment, he would "fight no more forever."

Gradually over the years the fame of father and son has become more appreciated, and monuments and plaques have been put up in their honor. In their beloved Wallowa Valley newcomers named a town for them, and a small park was established at the north end of Wallowa Lake where the elder Joseph was buried.

Another place honoring them is Joseph Canyon, twenty miles north of Enterprise, where the younger Joseph was born in a cave overlooking the creek and canyon. Originally the canyon was part of the 6.5 million-acre Nez Perce Reservation created in 1855, which was later taken away by the whites. At this writing, it is still an undesignated wilderness within the Wallowa-Whitman National Forest. Most of its western boundary is State 3, which runs between Clarkston, Washington, and Wallowa Lake. The Joseph Canyon Viewpoint is just off the highway. The canyon can be entered here but the trail is extremely steep for two miles. Nine miles south on State 3 is the trailhead for Davis Creek Trail, by far the best route into the 2,000-foot-deep Joseph Creek Canyon. The trail runs nearly ten miles north along Davis Creek until it joins Swamp Creek. Then the creek plunges into Joseph Canyon.

For more information:

Wallowa-Whitman National Forest, 1550 Dewey Avenue, Baker City, OR 97814. 503-523-6391.

Wallowa Valley Ranger District, Route 1, Box M, Enterprise, OR 97846. 503-432-2171.

6
Central Oregon

KLAMATH BASIN

Six National Wildlife Refuges — including the first to be established in America — are clustered around Klamath Falls, some in Oregon, some in California, and one that sits astride the border between the two states. They were created to preserve what remains of the shallow lakes and marshes that characterize the area. Originally about 185,000 acres were covered by these wetlands which each year attracted more than six million migratory waterfowl in addition to pelicans, cormorants, egrets, and herons. Less than 25 percent of the area remains today as a result of efforts by the Bureau of Reclamation to drain the lakes and marshes and convert them to agriculture.

Concerned about the dramatic loss of waterfowl habitat, the U.S. Fish and Wildlife Service was able to establish six refuges covering nearly 125,000 acres, and the Oregon Department of Fish and Wildlife added 2,400 acres with its Klamath Wildlife Area.

FISH HERDERS

White pelicans have wingspans of up to ten feet and may soar 100 miles away from the nest while foraging, leaving the mate to tend the nest on a protected island. Rather than diving for food like the brown pelican does, the whites often feed in groups. They form a "net" and drive fish to the center, then scoop them into their five-gallon gullets.

The refuges are in a beautiful setting on the edge of the Cascade Range, where it begins to wear down and flatten out before officially ending in Northern California. Low mountains surround them and the conical Mount McLoughlin is a visual anchor to the north. The refuges have a wide variety of habitats, including marshes, open water, grassy meadows, coniferous forests, sagebrush and juniper grasslands, land under cultivation by farmers, and rocky cliffs and slopes. Their success is evident from the 411 species of wildlife known to use them.

Most of the Klamath Basin's agricultural economy is based on land converted from wetlands to agriculture. The agricultural and

DLN 93©

A young bald eagle at home

water programs of the refuges, except for the state-managed Klamath Wildlife Area, are coordinated under an agreement between the U.S. Fish and Wildlife Service and the Bureau of Reclamation.

In spite of the reduced size of the marshes, the area still attracts most of the waterfowl that follow the Pacific Flyway; nearly one million arrive each year during the peak of the fall migration. This makes the Klamath Basin one of the most heavily used refuge systems in America.

The Lower Klamath National Wildlife Refuge, which straddles the Oregon-California border due south of Klamath Falls, was the first in America and was signed into existence by President Theodore Roosevelt in 1908. Covering 47,600 acres, it is a combination of shallow marshes, open water, crops, and grassy uplands. Its natural wetlands and the grains grown by farmers who lease the land provide food for both wintering and migrating waterfowl.

To reach the refuge, drive south from Klamath Falls on US 97 to State 161, which runs along the Oregon-California border and the northern edge of the refuge. Stop by headquarters to pick up a brochure with a marked auto-tour route through much of the area.

Three years after the Lower Klamath refuge was created, the 33,440-acre Clear Lake National Wildlife Refuge was added. It is due east of Lower Klamath and is wholly in California. It has 20,000 acres of water surface and its small islands provide nesting sites for pelicans, cormorants, and other colonial birds. The islands are off-limits, of course, but your binoculars or long lens will permit you to see some of the nests and the habitat.

Clear Lake is south of Tule Lake on State 139. Drive to the Clear Lake Reservoir Road and follow it northeast to the refuge.

Two more refuges were added to the cluster in 1928. The 38,908-acre Tule Lake refuge is mostly open water and croplands, of which 15,000 acres are leased to farmers under a Bureau of Reclamation program, and another 1,400 acres grow cereals and grains. Waste grain and potatoes are also distributed to the migratory birds.

Tule Lake is separated from the Lower Klamath refuge by the rugged Sheepy Ridge, and is reached by following the directions to Lower Klamath. The visitors center and headquarters are on Hill Road, which heads south from State 161 just east of Sheepy Ridge.

The other 1928 addition is the Upper Klamath refuge, on the north end of Upper Klamath Lake. The 14,376-acre refuge is marsh and open water with Mount McLoughlin towering behind. It is the most remote of the group and can be reached only by boat. Some marsh areas are closed from spring through fall to protect the nesting birds. It has a self-guided canoe trail, which makes this one of the most rewarding refuges in the system, for the birds pay less attention to a canoe than to someone approaching on foot.

Upper Klamath is reached via West Side Road, which splits off State 140 and runs north past the refuge to intersect with State 62.

Klamath Forest Refuge, encompassing 16,377 acres due north of Klamath Falls, was established in 1958, when it was purchased from the Klamath Indians. It is a large natural marsh that supports migratory waterfowl as well as raptors, shorebirds, and sandhill cranes. Several other species of birds and mammals live in the adjacent pine forests. The Silver Lake Highway intersects the refuge a

---

THE NATIONAL SYMBOL

Eagles mate for life and reach breeding age at four or five years. They establish their nesting territories in February and lay two or three eggs. Incubation lasts about thirty-five days and both birds share the egg-sitting duty. Eaglets are born in April and grow rapidly, requiring a lot of food. They learn to fly at about three months of age and usually leave the nest after the fourth month. Eaglets banded in the Klamath Basin have been found as far away as northern British Columbia and Mexico the same summer they left the nest. The majority remain in the Klamath area.

Oregon has the largest concentration of bald eagles in the forty-eight conterminous states, and the largest population is near Klamath Falls, where, during the 1980s, it was common for more than 500 eagles to winter in the area. The next largest concentration is along the upper Crooked River Valley where more than 100 eagles are seen each March.

short distance east of US 97, and driving through the refuge is, at times, almost like driving through a tunnel, for the marsh plants grow so tall.

Bear Valley refuge was added in 1978 to protect a major winter night-roost site for bald eagles. (Nearly 300 were counted there one evening.) The purchasing program is still under way and will eventually total 4,120 acres. The refuge, which also has stands of old-growth timber, is closed from November 1 through March 30 to protect the eagles while they are nesting there. The Bear Valley refuge is south of Klamath Falls just off US 97 at Worden.

Oregon's Klamath Wildlife Area covers 2,400 acres of open water, islands, and marshes six miles south of Klamath Falls between the Klamath River and US 97. It was created in 1949 as an addition to the refuges already in existence. Visitors are encouraged to stop at the National Wildlife Refuge headquarters for information and to shop in the cooperative association store. A percentage of the income from the sale of booklets and other wildlife preservation items supports interpretive and educational programs.

There's no "best" time to visit these refuges because each season has its own beauty, but the migratory spring months of March to June and the fall months of October to December usually yield the most birds. Refuges are open during daylight hours, except as modified by hunting regulations or complete closures during sensitive nesting periods. No overnight camping is permitted in any of them.

For more information:

Klamath Basin NWRs, Refuge Manager, Route 1, Box 74, Tulelake, CA 96134. 916-667-2231.

Klamath Wildlife Area, 1800 Miller Island Road, West, Klamath Falls, OR 97603. 503-883-5734.

Klamath County Visitors Association, P.O. Box 1867, Klamath Falls, OR 97601. 503-884-0666.

CRATER LAKE NATIONAL PARK

For reasons best known to politicians, Oregon, a state of extraordinary beauty, has only one national park. It has national monuments, national scenic areas, national recreation areas, and so forth, but only one place that has been granted national park status. But what a fantastic one Crater Lake National Park is.

When Mount St. Helens exploded in 1980, the world got an idea of what it must have been like 7,000 years ago when Mount Mazama had a series of violent eruptions before it finally imploded on itself, leaving hardly more than a hole in the ground where a 12,000-foot peak once stood. This hole in the ground in south-central Oregon is what we now know as Crater Lake.

Throughout the Northwest, especially north and east of the mountain, geologists have identified a telltale layer of ash from the mountain that spread for thousands of miles. That final cataclysmic event seems to have been the last gasp of the volcano, because for the next 5,000 years, the almost perfectly round caldera gradually filled with water. At 1,932 feet it is the deepest lake in the United States and the sixth deepest in the world. The lake has no outlet, but through rain and snow accumulation in the winter followed by evaporation during the rest of the year, the water level seldom varies more than three feet over the course of a year.

The volcano and resulting lake figure prominently in the legends of the Native Americans who lived in the area. They believed it was a battleground for two feuding gods, and when the lake formed, some shamans forbade their followers to look at it. Other shamans preached that its water held healing or supernatural properties. Because of these strong beliefs, the local tribes didn't tell pioneers of its existence, and Europeans lived in the area for more than half a century before a party of prospectors found it in 1853, while searching for the Lost Cabin gold mine.

The lake immediately fascinated the settlers, who found that it was virtually devoid of life. In 1886 the U.S. Geological Survey organized a large party to explore the lake by a boat, which had to be carried to it. Weighing about 1,000 pounds, the boat required thirty-five men and sixty-five horses and mules to be transported through the forest and up the mountain to the lake.

The explorers, like visitors today, were struck by the intense blue color of the water, which is the result of deep penetration of light into the water — up to 300 feet at Crater Lake, which makes it the clearest lake in America. As further evidence of the light's penetration, moss has been found growing 325 feet down. It receives up to forty-five feet of snow during normal winters but seldom freezes, because it has stored heat from the summer sun.

The park has built a thirty-three-mile, mostly one-way road encircling the rim of Crater Lake, and it must be driven clockwise. All buildings are clustered at Rim Village at the park entrance on the southwest side, including the visitors center, a cafeteria, park head-quarters, and the aging and rustic Crater Lake Lodge.

Several trails lead off the rim drive to viewpoints. Most are short; only one or two are more than two miles long. The Pacific Crest Trail runs west of the lake with a spur trail leading down to Rim Village. Rangers conduct campfire programs every night during the summer and lead snowshoe hikes (snowshoes provided) during the winter. A concessionaire offers boat tours with a stop at Wizard Island, an eerie volcanic pinnacle. The park is open year-round, but the rim drive is closed during the winter.

For more information:

Crater Lake National Park, P.O. Box 7, Crater Lake, OR 97604. 503-594-2211.

Crater Lake Lodge Company, P.O. Box 97, Crater Lake, OR 97604. 503-594-2511. (Also has information on boat tours.)

JOHN DAY FOSSIL BEDS NATIONAL MONUMENT

No matter what you read in this or other books or in National Park Service brochures, none of it will prepare you for the colors you are going to see — bands upon bands of color. And if you are fortunate enough to visit the monument at the height of the spring flowers season, you will wonder if you haven't stumbled onto the set of a movie being made about someone's intense memories. The fossil beds, especially in the Painted Hills Unit, are unlike any other place I've seen in America; and when you drive away from them, you may wonder for a moment, as I did, if you really saw what you think you saw.

In addition to this spectacular spring display, the hills have a more lasting story to tell: More than forty-five million years of planetary history are recorded in this multicolored, three-part national monument. The fossils of plants and mammals found here in the loose soil of rolling hills are a record of the Cenozoic era, the most recent geologic era, which lasted from about fifty million years ago until only five million years ago.

When the fossilized plants and animals were alive, the Cascade Range had not been formed and the whole area was tropical, humid, practically a rain forest, with 100 or more inches of annual rainfall. Ferns, avocados, palms, and other tropical vegetation grew rampantly.

The uplifting of the Cascades and the Coast Range turned the area into a desert. Succeeding volcanic eruptions deposited several feet of multicolored ash and dust, and heavy rains created mudflows that covered plants and mammals alike. This was followed by the steady accumulation of wind-blown soil (*loess*) that further covered the land.

While the whole area contains fossils – you may dig for them at a variety of places, but *never* inside the national monument – the monument has restricted itself to three sites: the Sheep Rock Unit, Painted Hills Unit, and Clarno Unit.

The cliffs at John Day

The Sheep Rock Unit is eight miles west of Dayville on US 26 and two miles north on State 19. It has the visitors center for the whole monument — rangers work out of temporary modular offices at the other two sites. Several short, easy walking trails have been built here with views of the colorful hills and exposed fossils. The Foree loop trail leads past blue-green claystone outcroppings and mammal fossils. The Island in Time Trail also has a wide variety of fossils and colorful claystone.

The Painted Hills Unit is west of Sheep Rock and a short distance from the town of Mitchell. If you have seen photographs of the monument, they probably were taken here, where you'll find the gracefully rounded mounds with layer upon layer of color and wildflowers covering the valley floor. A driving route takes you to an overlook and to individual fossil beds, but the most rewarding trail is the three-mile High Desert Trail, which lets you get away from the crowds and up close to the multicolored hills.

The Clarno Unit, a considerable distance from the others, is on State 218 almost due north of the Painted Hills. It is reached by driving north on State 207 to State 19. Follow State 19 northwest to the town of Fossil, then turn west on State 218. Clarno has a large selection of petrified logs and branches, a natural arch, and a picnic area.

For more information:

John Day Fossil Beds National Monument, 420 West Main Street, John Day, OR 97845. 503-575-0721.

Cant Ranch Visitors Center, Sheep Rock. 503-934-2801.

NEWBERRY NATIONAL VOLCANIC MONUMENT

While Oregon has an abundance of beaches, evergreen trees, world-class croplands, and swift rivers, it also has an abundance of torturous, barren landscapes. There probably are more square miles of horizontal basalt here than in any other state, excepting Hawaii. Much of the central part of Oregon was composed of volcanic eruptions, ranging from the explosions of Mount Mazama to fissures that opened in the earth so molten rock could ooze out and spread across the landscape like a hot-oil spill.

Some people are depressed, or at least very unimpressed, by landscapes devoid of trees and most plants; but the more fortunate travelers find a beauty in all natural things, as they will in this newest (established in 1990) of Oregon's national monuments. It covers 56,000 acres in the Deschutes National Forest southeast of Bend and is something of a classroom for students of volcanic action and geothermal activity.

The Lava Lands Visitors Center serves as the monument's headquarters and is ten miles south of Bend on US 97. It has dioramas, displays of things found in the monument, books, and brochures.

Just north of the visitors center is Lava Butte, a 500-foot, perfectly shaped cinder cone with a trail leading to the summit. It was created about 6,000 years ago as lava bombs and cinders were burped up by a volcanic vent and fell around it and cooled.

Most of the main features are south of the visitors center. Follow US 97 south to State 21, head east for about fifteen miles to Paulina and East Lakes in the center of the lava flows. Just south of Paulina Lake is Big Obsidian Flow, one of the largest obsidian flows in the world. You can pick up pieces of obsidian and see how smooth they are, but be careful: obsidian is extremely sharp — so sharp, in fact, that it is sometimes used for delicate surgical procedures.

Lava River Cave, near the Lava Lands Visitors Center, is a lava tube more than a mile long, with a ceiling high enough to walk in. The cave remains at a constant temperature in the upper thirties, so dress accordingly. Lanterns can be rented at a modest charge from the ranger on site.

Newberry Crater, actually twin lakes, is something like Crater Lake except that after the lake was formed, more volcanic activity divided the crater into the two lakes of today, Paulina and East lakes. The crater is all that remains of Mount Newberry, which had a base diameter of twenty-five miles and is believed to have stood about 20,000 feet before it collapsed in on itself.

The visitors center is open May through October.

For more information:

Lava Lands Visitors Center, 1645 US 20 East, Bend, OR 97701. 503-382-5668.

Deschutes National Forest (same address as above). 503-388-2715.

Bend Chamber of Commerce, 63085 North US 97, Bend, OR 97701. 503-382-3221.

DESCHUTES RIVER CANYON

Several years ago when the first inflatable boats came on the market I bought an inflatable canoe that was supposed to be safe on the calmest of lakes and the whitest of white-water rivers. My first test with it came on the Deschutes River between Madras and Maupin. It was not a happy test: Riding in it was almost as tricky as trying to stand on a floating log. The very first riffle flipped me out, and it took the first real rapid only one bump to put me back in the water. For the rest of the trip through the desert canyons I walked around all rapids and lined the canoe through.

That series of mishaps introduced me to one of the most beautiful rivers in the West. The Deschutes seems designed for white-water lovers because it has sets of rapids strategically placed so that

A rough-legged hawk

at least twice a day you will have an adrenalin rush. The rest of the river is a series of quiet pools (where fat trout watch every tempting morsel with distrust) and riffles (where younger, less experienced trout lurk behind rocks and tree roots, not usually so fussy about what they put into their mouths).

Most of the west bank of the river here borders the Warm Springs Indian Reservation, and entry is prohibited. The eastern side is a combination of government and private land. The river will never be placed in a wilderness category because railroad tracks follow it through the rugged canyons from the Columbia River to Madras and beyond to Bend.

Oddly, there were two railroads along the river at one time, one on both sides, when James J. Hill and Edward Harriman had a bitter battle over whose railroad would serve the area. Hill won. As a result of this controversy, it seems that just when you have settled down for the night after a day of drifting, fishing, cooking, eating, and telling tall tales, along comes a freight train with a horn-happy engineer.

The fifty-one-mile stretch of river from Maupin downstream to the Columbia River has been added to the State Scenic Waterway system, but the river upstream to Madras is equally beautiful. It flows through barren desert landscape where less than ten inches of rainfall is the average. Several mountains and bluffs line the river and turn a brilliant red and yellow in the evening sun. Except for the railroad, the Deschutes is quite remote most of the way down to Maupin, with snug campsites along its bank.

Drifting the section from Maupin to the Columbia requires a Deschutes River Boater Pass, which can be bought at any sporting goods store. Fishing is not permitted from boats anywhere on the river.

We put in at a railroad siding called South Junction, at the end of a dirt road off US 197, and drifted to a campsite just below White-horse Rapids. (We were there when the spring salmon fly hatch occurred, which is the one time of the year rainbow trout practice gluttony.) Below Whitehorse, we drifted between soaring canyon walls and flat-topped mountains, then ran through Dant Chute, a sudden drop in the river that is something like riding a roller coaster.

Our trip ended just above Maupin, where we had dropped a car on the way in. (You can usually find someone to drive your car to the place you intend to leave the river by checking first with the Chamber of Commerce.)

I've never floated the lower Deschutes but hope to. It is a much wilder river than the upper stretch and has everything, including Sherars Falls, which boaters must portage around. For about five miles beyond Sherars Falls are some of the heaviest rapids of the river, which must be scouted before they are attempted. After that comes more than thirty miles of calm water through desert canyon country. The last six miles have a series of rapids before the river flattens and dies in the backwaters of The Dalles Dam on the Columbia River.

For more information:

Oregon Parks and Recreation Division, 525 Trade Street S.E., Salem, OR 97310. 503-378-6305.

Bureau of Land Management, Prineville District, 185 East 4th Street, Prineville, OR 97754. 503-447-4115.

Maupin Chamber of Commerce, P.O. Box 220, Maupin, OR 97037. 503-395-2599.

Madras Chamber of Commerce, 197 S.E. 5th Street, Madras, OR 97741. 503-475-6975.

CROOKED RIVER NATIONAL GRASSLAND

When we think of the Dust Bowl destruction, we generally think of the Great Plains, especially Texas, Oklahoma, and Kansas, but that same drought, combined with poor farming techniques, was equally devastating in Oregon. All along the eastern slopes of the Cascade Range and into the desert, dirt blew into the doors and windows of abandoned homesteads. Broken farming equipment, rickety windmills, and children's toys were scattered across the landscape.

Much of the property was taken over by the Federal Land Banks and commercial banks – 35 percent had suffered that fate by

1935. The federal government passed the Resettlement Administration and Bankhead-Jones Farm Tenant Act and under it bought land from the few remaining homesteaders.

In central Oregon hundreds of homesteaders on thousands of acres of land were bought out and the land was first placed under the supervision of the Soil Conservation Service; then in 1954 it was transferred to the forest service. A restoration project called the Central Oregon Land Utilization Project was begun, and in 1960 it became the Crooked River National Grassland – one of only nineteen national grasslands in America. The forest service's orders are to administer it "under sound and progressive principles of land conservation and multiple use."

Crooked River National Grassland has a total of 173,629 acres of which 111,379 are under forest service supervision. The remaining land is in private ownership or is publicly owned land administered by the Bureau of Land Management, the State of Oregon, or Jefferson County. It is administered by the Ochoco National Forest as a ranger district.

The grassland is one of the less noticeable preservation projects in Oregon. It doesn't have the distinct boundaries of a national park or a wilderness area. To be honest, I have driven through it dozens of times without even knowing it existed, and I might never have noticed its existence had I not written this book. The grassland encompasses three large towns – Madras, Culver, and Metolius – and two major highways – US 97 and US 26 – plus many smaller roads. Thus it is a prime example of the multiple-use concept.

One major reason for its existence is to be sure that the land, most of which is of marginal use, is never subjected to poor farming practices again. It is land that never should have been plowed, and much of the forest service's efforts over the past forty-five years has been either restoring native vegetation or at least introducing vegetation that is compatible with the soil. This includes crested and beardless wheatgrass; attempts to restore native bluebunch wheatgrass were unsuccessful. The homestead era was so devastating to native plants that it is impossible to determine exactly what grasses originally grew here, but researchers believe bluebunch wheatgrass,

Idaho fescue, sagebrush, rabbitbrush, bitterbrush, and juniper were indigenous to the area.

Livestock is permitted to graze on the land under an allotment program with the Gray Butte Grazing Association, formed by local stockmen who hire range riders to tend the cattle, maintain reservoirs and fences, and take care of other chores.

The area is popular for recreation and has three lakes with boating, camping, swimming, and fishing for trout, crappie, bass, bluegill, and catfish. Most recently kokanee, the landlocked salmon, has been introduced to some lakes.

Simtustus Lake on the Deschutes River covers 637 acres. It was named by the Warm Springs tribe to honor a warrior who was a scout for the U.S. Army in the 1867–68 campaign against the Paiutes. The dam was built primarily for electrical power but also serves as a holding reservoir for Billy Chinook Lake upstream.

Billy Chinook Lake on the Deschutes covers 3,916 acres and was also built for hydroelectric power. It has many boat-launching sites, swimming beaches, and camping and picnic sites.

Haystack Reservoir, on Haystack Creek, covers only 282 acres and is used to store water for irrigation projects. It has been stocked with rainbow trout, largemouth bass, and crappies, and fishing is easy from both boats and the shoreline. Lodging is available at a private resort and the forest service campground.

The weather is usually sunny and the temperatures are generally moderate; however, the elevations from 2,000 to 5,000 feet make many evenings chilly throughout the year. Rainfall averages only 10.5 inches, but violent electrical storms may occur during the spring and summer months.

For more information:

Crooked River National Grassland, Ochoco National Forest, 3000 East Third, Prineville, OR 97754. 503-447-9640.

7
Oregon Desert

STEENS MOUNTAIN
AND MALHEUR NATIONAL WILDLIFE REFUGE

Of all the place names in southeastern Oregon, few are better known or more beloved than Steens Mountain and the lakes around it, particularly Malheur Lake. Steens Mountain is only thirty miles long, but it stands alone on the high desert and is not part of a mountain range.

Its 9,670-foot elevation is diminished somewhat because the surrounding desert floor is at the 4,500-foot level. But that 5,000 feet is sufficient to give Steens Mountain its own climate. Its summit can have freezing weather in the middle of summer, and snow has fallen on it in every month of the year. While the desert floor gets only about seven inches of rainfall a year, the summit averages about thirty-two inches and supports a hearty plant population. It attracts bad weather and is a lightning rod for electrical storms. Indeed, a creek at its base was named Donner und Blitzen by an early traveler because he camped there during a thunder and lightning storm.

Steens Mountain stands like an island in the great sea of alkali flats and sagebrush, and its upper reaches are unlike anything else for miles in all directions. It was formed as a fault — it is one of the largest fault blocks in the world — with the west side sloping upward in a series of dips and pitches. The eastern side is a sheer drop-off to the flat Alvord Desert a mile below.

It is a popular study site for geologists and naturalists because its history is so easily read in the landscape. It has four large U-shaped gorges — Kiger, Little Blitzen, Big Indian, and Wild Horse —

that were scooped out by glaciers during the Ice Age. On top are hanging valleys, which were created by glaciers pushing dirt and rocks ahead of them, then melting to leave giant depressions behind the earthen dams.

The seasons move up the mountainside gradually, and bees and hummingbirds ascend with the blossoming wildflowers. This migration of the seasons plus the various soil formations have created belts of plant life that can be seen as you drive on the self-guided tour. It begins with sagebrush at the base, moves into juniper, then quaking aspen.

If the mountain has a "signature" animal, it would be the prong-horn antelope. This animal can run fifty miles an hour in short bursts and is seen at all elevations of the mountain. An interesting note about pronghorns: They are one of very few horned animals that shed their horns each year. The horny outer sheath is lost, the bony core remains. Both bucks and does have horns. Other species include mule deer, Rocky Mountain elk, and a variety of smaller mammals, including badgers and various rodents such as field mice.

The mountain also supports a herd of wild horses that have been there for decades — since their ancestors escaped from early settlers. The Bureau of Land Management (BLM) keeps the herd at

An Oregon great egret at Malheur Lake

about 300 head, allowing them to roam free. Those captured here and on other BLM-managed land are held in corrals near Burns. You can arrange for a tour of the corrals by calling the headquarters at the number listed below.

Steens Mountain is under the management of the Bureau of Land Management, which maintains a sixty-six-mile loop road open from July 1 through October 31, snow conditions permitting. Be aware that the road is rough, steep, and narrow, and has no guard-rails. It turns off State 205 at Frenchglen and returns to the highway a few miles south of Frenchglen. The road is described in a BLM publication as the highest in Oregon.

A few miles northwest of the mountain is the Malheur National Wildlife Refuge. It is part of the Steens Mountain experience but is managed by the Fish and Wildlife Service. The refuge covers 185,000 acres of marshes, meadows, and several man-made ponds, and was created to protect birds that use it for nesting and as a stop on their migratory path. Among these species are Canada geese, avocets, teals, mallards, white pelicans, greater sandhill cranes, shorebirds, trumpeter swans, and pheasants. It also provides a home for fifty-seven species of mammals.

The refuge includes Malheur and Harney lakes, two very large but shallow bodies of water surrounded by marshes and subject to shifts in climate. In recent memory they were in danger of drying up completely, then two or three years later threatened to flood State 205, which passes between them.

Before the turn of the century the lakes and marshes were so filled with birds that the first white men there were stunned by the volume. One early visitor wrote that local Native Americans would go into the marshes amid the birds by hiding behind a pony, then shoot an arrow into their midst and sometimes kill as many as three birds that way.

During this period the feathers of snowy egrets were prized for hats. Hunters would shoot the adult egrets when they returned to their nests to feed the young. Consequently, the young birds would then die of starvation. President Theodore Roosevelt put a stop to this in 1908 when, at the urging of local conservationists, he set aside the area as a refuge.

No camping is permitted in Malheur National Wildlife Refuge, but it is permitted at the Malheur Field Station and several locations around Steens Mountain. The BLM has fee campgrounds at Page Springs, Fish Lake, and Jackman Park along the loop route, and there is a private campground at Frenchglen. The Frenchglen Hotel, owned by Oregon State Parks, has eight rooms and serves breakfast and dinner. Other lodging is available nearby and is listed below.

For more information:

Bureau of Land Management, Burns District, HC 74, 12553 US 20 West, Hines, OR 97738. 503-573-5241.

Malheur National Wildlife Refuge, HC 72, Box 245, Princeton, OR 97721. 503-493-2612.

Malheur Field Station, HC 72, Box 260, Princeton, OR 97721. 503-493-2629.

Steens Mountain Resort (a private campground), Frenchglen, OR 97736. 503-493-2415.

Frenchglen Hotel, Frenchglen, OR 97736. 503-493-2825.

Hotel Diamond, Box 10, Diamond, OR 97722. 503-493-1898.

McCoy Creek Inn, HC 72, Box 1, Diamond, OR 97722. 503-493-2131.

HART MOUNTAIN NATIONAL ANTELOPE REFUGE, WARNER VALLEY, AND ABERT RIM

More remote and less developed than Malheur and Steens Mountain, this 275,000-acre refuge covers Poker Jim Flat and almost all of Hart Mountain, plus a series of shallow lakes at the base of the mountain and several square miles of sagebrush desert. Hart Mountain Refuge was established in 1936 to provide spring, summer, and fall range for the antelope herds, which usually winter east of the refuge in the Catlow Valley.

After the refuge was established, biologists found a greater diversity of animal and plant life than expected, so its purpose was expanded to include all life-forms native to the area. This includes

Bighorn sheep square off at Hart Mountain

more than 330 species of wildlife and numerous plants, and the refuge most recently added a native-plants display at its headquarters to show the interrelationship between all living things there. Some of the more dominant plants are in the display: basin wild rye, taper-tip hawksbeard, Indian ryegrass, low sagebrush, rough fescue, Idaho fescue, arrowleaf balsamroot, bluebunch wheatgrass, and bitterbrush.

Hart Mountain, like Steens Mountain, is a fault block. Its highest point is 8,065 feet above sea level but the floor of Warner Valley on the west side is just over 5,000 feet. The mountain has several good springs plus a hot spring where visitors may camp and bathe.

Wildlife viewing is the most popular activity on the refuge. In addition to the speedy antelope, California bighorn sheep have been established on Poker Jim Ridge, at the northern end of the mountain. Mule deer, coyotes, bobcats, jackrabbits, cottontails, marmots, and ground squirrels also live there. More than 260 species of birds have been recorded and the refuge visitors center, open twenty-four hours a day, has a wildlife brochure which lists them.

This is also a good place for rockhounding. The refuge has a daily limit of seven pounds of rocks with restrictions on removing artifacts (such as arrowheads) and bans on digging or blasting.

The refuge boundary goes only to the bottom of the mountain in Warner Valley and does not include the Warner Lakes, which can be seen from the road as it descends from Poker Jim Ridge. These lakes, like Malheur and Harney, rise and fall with the fluctuations in climate. From above, they look otherworldly, like enormous pieces of tile fitted in a table. They range in color from deep blue to that blinding white only alkali can produce. Seeing them from above is one of the most interesting sights on the refuge.

The headquarters are beside Rock Creek, almost in the center of the refuge, twenty-eight miles of rough road from Frenchglen and twenty-five miles by both paved and gravel road to Plush. The nearest visitors facilities are sixty-five miles away in Lakeview.

Abert Rim is included in this chapter because it is connected to Hart Mountain and the Warner Lakes and forms the western boundary of Warner Valley. Seen from the valley, Abert Rim looks like any other low mountain in the desert, but its seemingly normal rise on the eastern side is dramatically different from the western side.

A fault scarp, the western face rises straight up, 4,000 feet off the valley floor, which makes it one of the highest fault scarps in North America; some signs say it is the highest. Before the fault began pushing this section of the earth upward to permit a Teutonic plate to slide beneath it, the whole area was absolutely flat. But subterranean volcanic action created hot springs and geysers in the region. The changing climate has caused the level of Lake Abert to rise and fall dramatically, from a depth of more than 2,000 feet during the Ice Ages to its present level of only a few feet. Indeed, during especially dry years the lake dries up entirely, leaving a white residue of alkali and other minerals as evidence of its existence.

The summit of Abert Rim can be reached by rough dirt roads from the eastern side, and is a popular place for hang gliding, which is not permitted in the Hart Mountain refuge.

For more information:

Hart Mountain National Antelope Refuge, P.O. Box 111, Lakeview, OR 97630. 503-947-3315.

Lake County Chamber of Commerce, 513 Center Street, Lakeview, OR 97630. 503-947-6040.

LOST FOREST

This 9,000-acre forest of ponderosa pine is perhaps the most unusual one in Oregon. It sits amid sand dunes in Christmas Valley, in an area where the annual rainfall is ten inches or less, more than forty miles from the nearest timber, and yet it continues to thrive. The Bureau of Land Management has set the forest aside as a Research Natural Area, which prevents it from being logged off and can be studied further for possible wilderness designation. So far the forest has yielded some unusual information to botanists. They have found that the ponderosa here have gone through genetic mutations to adapt to the harsh surroundings. One mutation has changed the genetic character of its seeds, which now germinate much more quickly than do other ponderosa pines.

The roots also have adapted to the unusual conditions. While other ponderosa need at least fourteen inches of annual rainfall, this forest has learned to survive on ten inches with the help of the soil composition. Although the forest floor is almost entirely sand, the sand sits atop a layer of hardpan that prevents moisture from passing through it. The sand retains the moisture, like a mulch, and the trees get much more of it than they normally would.

Studies of tree rings have shown that two of the worst droughts occurred in 1920 and 1936, the years that drove nearly every homesteader from the Oregon desert into more fertile valleys. In spite of the harsh growing conditions, the largest juniper in Oregon was found in the Lost Forest, with a trunk more than eighteen feet in circumference.

Much of the forest was logged during pioneer years for fence posts, building materials, and firewood. Commercial logging occurred in the 1950s, but the forest is closed to cutting today.

The Lost Forest is part of a scientific and recreational complex gradually developing in the Christmas Valley area. To enter it, you pass through a 10,000-acre stretch of sand dunes, some sixty feet high. Nearby are a series of dramatic lava flows, cinder cones, a crack in the basalt nearly two miles long and forty feet wide, lava tubes, and Fort Rock — the remnant of a cinder cone shaped like an amphitheater, which has been made into a state park.

The Lost Forest is fascinating but not especially user-friendly for the self-propelled outdoorsman. You may find it to be one of those places you are glad exists but not feel compelled to visit often. It has but a few primitive campsites scattered among the trees and absolutely no water. The sand blows with virtually every breath of air, adding grit to your food, and walking in it is a chore.

To reach the Lost Forest, drive east of the town of Christmas Valley on the paved highway that leads to Wagontire. After about nine miles watch for a sign to the forest, sand dunes, and Fossil Lake. Head north on that road for another fifteen miles, the last one or two of which track over the sand dunes. This is not a good place to visit during the rainy season in winter and spring, and is always risky with the family sedan, because if you get stuck in the sand, you may sit there for hours before another car arrives.

For more information:

Bureau of Land Management, Lakeview Resource Area, P.O. Box 151, Lakeview, OR 97630. 503-947-2177.

OWYHEE NATIONAL SCENIC WATERWAY

The Owyhee River is Oregon's most remote river. It also has the most exciting white water in the state, although this is limited to only April and May, when the river has enough water to safely run the rapids. The rest of the year the deep, picturesque canyons of the Owyhee are silent, except for an occasional desert backpacker or a cattleman checking on his herd.

The Owyhee is down in the far southeastern corner of the state where only one highway goes through. A few ranchers' roads wander through the region, but it is such rugged going that most of the land lies ignored. There's a good reason for this: The region has some of the roughest landscape in the West, thanks to the enormous lava flows that covered the land. After the lava hardened, it cracked and broke into a maze of sharp rocks and broken sheets of basalt, making much of the area virtually unapproachable. If you have traveled through Volcanoes National Park on the island of Hawaii, you will understand how rugged the Jordan Valley and the Owyhee River Canyon are.

The river was named in honor of two Hawaiians (Owyhee was originally the correct spelling of the islands) who worked for a beaver trapper and were killed by Indians in 1819. In spite of the inhospitable area, campsites found in caves and other records of human presence date back at least 12,000 years. Perhaps the area was selected because it was so far removed from other tribes, the distance and terrible landscape making it too much trouble for others to bother the river inhabitants.

Hardy backpackers have several routes along the river that range from two to three miles and up to twenty-five to thirty miles. Some are from road's end down to the river canyon and others are through the canyon at low-water periods.

Most people go to the Owyhee for the beautiful and thrilling float trips it offers. The most popular is the sixty-three miles from the small town of Rome on US 95 to the reservoir behind Owyhee Dam. When the dam was built in the 1930s, it created what was then Oregon's biggest irrigation project, but it wasn't until the 1950s that adventurers made the first float trip down it to the take-out ramp at Leslie Gulch on the reservoir.

The trip takes four or five days, and includes rapids up to Class 4, which dictates a portage. Safety is extremely important here because the 1,000-foot canyon is so remote and has no roads. If you should lose your equipment here, you will have a long and lonely walk for help.

Also, the river temperature is very cold during spring runoff, and since Oregon's desert is so high (Rome is at the 3,300-foot level), the weather can be especially cold during the spring, so you should dress accordingly.

The river has four major rapids and an abandoned dam made of rocks. All are runable but caution is urged and all should be scouted before attempting. After the river dies in the dam back-waters, you are left with about eight miles to row or paddle to the takeout at Leslie Gulch, not the easiest thing to do with an inflatable raft. If you are facing into a stiff breeze, you might as well pull over and camp until the wind shifts in your favor.

You can take another float trip on the upper Owyhee River, a thirty-five-mile gauntlet that has more white water and more danger than the Rome-to-Leslie Gulch trip. This one begins at a river crossing a long, hard drive south from Jordan Valley to a place called Three Forks, where North and Middle forks of the Owyhee join forces.

The run has several rapids that require portaging, and all are potentially dangerous. Perhaps the worst is a ten-foot waterfall named the Widowmaker. Not only is this Class 5 cataract dangerous itself, it is preceded by half a mile of Class 3 rapids, which tend to fill your boat with water, making it difficult to maneuver or even pull to shore. This is the worst of several rough sets of rapids that make the river a popular challenge for white-water rafters and kayakers.

No permits are required to float the Owyhee, but it is strongly recommended that you register with the Bureau of Land Management office so someone will know where you are.

If running wild rivers and hiking across inhospitable terrain are not of interest, the geologic features here are sure to capture your attention. The area is so contorted by volcanic activities that it could serve as a geology classroom. Jordan Valley was created by a series of volcanic eruptions and lava flows, which resulted in sandwiches of lava, ash, and soil layers that can be seen on hillsides and along the Owyhee River. The lava formations are of great interest to geologists and volcanologists because the valley is laced with lava tubes, spatter cones, vents, fault zones, miles-long cracks in the surface, pressure ridges, domes, and virtually every kind of lava flow that exists.

Fossils of pre-Spanish horses, camels, antelopes, bears, and other mammals have been discovered here. Rockhounders love the area, too, because petrified wood, thunder eggs, agates, and other precious stones can be found in outcroppings amid the basaltic wasteland.

For more information:
Bureau of Land Management, Vale District, 100 Oregon Street, Vale, OR 97918. 503-473-3144.

Appendix

OREGON'S ENDANGERED AND THREATENED WILDLIFE SPECIES

(By way of definition, an endangered species is in immediate danger of extinction in all or a large part of its range. A threatened species is in slightly better shape but may become endangered in all or a large part of its range.)

Endangered

Fish: Borax Lake chub.

Reptiles: Green sea turtle, leatherback sea turtle.

Birds: Short-tailed albatross, brown pelican, Aleutian Canada goose, American peregrine falcon, California least tern.

A bewhiskered sea otter on the endangered list

Mammals: Gray wolf, gray whale, sei whale, sperm whale, blue whale, humpback whale, black right whale, fin whale, Columbian white-tailed deer.

Threatened
Fish: Hutton Spring tui chub, Foskett Spring speckled dace, Warner sucker.

Reptiles: Pacific Ridley sea turtle, loggerhead sea turtle.

Birds: Bald eagle, northern spotted owl, Arctic peregrine falcon, western snowy plover.

Mammals: Kit fox, wolverine, sea otter.

Source: Oregon Department of Fish and Wildlife.

AVOIDING HYPOTHERMIA

Nearly every year someone dies of hypothermia in Oregon, and it isn't only in winter; hypothermia is one of the leading causes of death during the summer months. Here is a common scenario: A group goes on a day hike in the mountains; rain begins falling and the wind blows. Someone in the group doesn't have rain gear and isn't able to get dry and warm. He or she begins shivering uncontrollably, becomes disoriented, falls asleep, and never wakes up.

Avoiding hypothermia should be a top priority while enjoying the outdoors, and it is simple to do: Stay dry and out of the wind. Take clothing suitable for the worst weather expected, which means rain gear, spare warm socks, and an extra shirt and pants. If you are unable to stay dry and warm, get out of the wind, build a fire, and drink warm liquids. If you don't have the proper clothing and can't build a suitable shelter, keep moving to generate body heat.

ESSENTIALS FOR WINTER TRAVEL

Be sure to tell friends or family members exactly where you are going. Mark your route on a map and leave it with them, and always call them when you return.

Include the following when you pack:
Topographic map and compass.
Flashlight and spare alkaline batteries.
Matches, firestarter, and good knife.
Extra food and water.
Ski or snowshoe repair kit.
Wool or synthetic clothing that wicks moisture while retaining its insulating properties, and an extra change of clothes.
Waterproof parka and rain pants.
Ground insulation, preferably a closed-cell foam pad to keep you off the snow.
First-aid kit, sunglasses, and sunscreen.
Avalanche rescue beacons, avalanche probes and shovels, if traveling in avalanche terrain.

NORDIC SKI TRAIL ETIQUETTE

When skiing in a track, give the downhill skier the right of way.
Do not go on cross-country tracks with snowmobiles and snowshoes because they damage the tracks.
Ask permission before entering private property.
Pack out all trash, even fruit peels.
Avoid disturbing wild animals. Stay out of known elk and deer wintering areas. If you see a wild animal, quietly detour around it.
Stay well away from established travel routes for personal sanitary needs.

WALKING SOFTLY

Keep your group small. Large groups tend to multiply damage to the wilderness, and they can be disruptive to others. (Groups entering a designated wilderness area must be no larger than twelve people and twelve head of stock.)
"In years past we spoke of wilderness survival as the ability of people to survive the wilderness. Now we speak of wilderness

survival as the land's ability to survive people." This statement by the forest service sums up the problem of people and wilderness throughout the world, and each of us can keep the human impact on wilderness low by using common sense and common courtesy. It is called the "No Trace" technique and includes these rules:

Stay on designated trails – never short-cut switchbacks.

When traveling cross-country, spread out and try to avoid wet meadows and fragile areas.

Never mark or blaze your route. Let others experience the challenge of finding their way as you did.

When meeting horses on the trail, step to the lower side of the trail to allow them to pass.

When camping:

Avoid open areas and select well-drained sites away from water and trails.

Choose well-established campsites if you must use popular areas.

Avoid trenching around tents.

Some areas have special setback regulations to prevent damage.

Avoid building campfires. Many high-use areas suffer from the effects of campfires and wood gathering.

Use a lightweight cookstove instead of a fire.

If you must have a campfire:

Use an existing fire ring unless it is near water or a trail.

Keep your fire small. Burn only small sticks that can be broken by hand. (Leave your ax and saw at home.)

Never cut live trees or dead snags.

Do not build fires within 100 feet of lakes, streams, and trails (all wildernesses). Some areas have special campfire setbacks.

Never leave a fire unattended and make sure your fire is dead out before you leave.

Pack out all plastic, foil, and glass. Don't try to burn it.

Sanitation:

Bathe and wash 200 feet from all water surfaces.

Use only small amounts of biodegradable soaps.

Bury human waste 200 feet from water in a "cat hole" no more than eight inches deep.

Bury fish entrails using the "cat hole" method. Never throw them into lakes or streams.

Never bury trash. Animals dig it up.

Pack it in, pack it out. Don't leave litter behind.

Backcountry courtesy:

Keep noise level down. Leave radios and tape players at home.

Keep pets under control at all times.

Never pick wildflowers or hack on trees or shrubs.

Never shoot firearms around lakes, streams, trails, or campsites.

Take only pictures. Leave with only fond memories.

And remember:

Permits are required for the Mount Jefferson, Mount Washington, and Three Sisters Wildernesses. Self-issue day-use permits are available at all wilderness trailheads. Overnight permits are available at selected commercial outlets or by mail, by phone, or in person at forest service offices.

You can occasionally see elk in Oregon wilderness areas.

TIPS FOR VIEWING WILDLIFE

Be quiet. Quick movements and loud noises will scare birds and animals. Your car or boat is a good blind and you may see more by remaining in the vehicle.

Be patient. Entering an area by car, boat, or on foot may initially disturb wildlife, but usually it will return if it doesn't feel threatened.

Visiting too many sites in one day may be disappointing, so allow plenty of time for each visit.

Take binoculars or spotting scopes so you can view better from a distance.

Use field guides to help identify wildlife. Most refuges also have a checklist of species common to the area.

Take a trip with naturalists or professional wildlife guides because they will know the area and can help you spot the wildlife.

Respect the wildlife and try to avoid disturbing it. They will stay only in areas in which they feel secure.

Don't feed or try to pet wildlife.

Avoid nesting areas in the spring.

Stay within designated areas to avoid disturbing wildlife or wandering onto private land.

Don't remove plants or animals.

Resources

Bend Chamber of Commerce, 63085 North US 97, Bend, OR 97701. 503-382-3221.

Bureau of Land Management, Burns District, HC 74, 12553 US 20 W, Hines, OR 97738. 503-573-5241.

Bureau of Land Management, Lakeview Resource Area, P.O. Box 151, Lakeview, OR 97630. 503-947-2177.

Bureau of Land Management, Prineville District, 185 East 4th Street, Prineville, OR 97754. 503-447-4115.

Cape Perpetua Scenic Area, P.O. Box 274, Yachats, OR 97498. 503-547-3289.

Columbia River Gorge National Scenic Area, 902 Wasco Avenue, Suite 200, Hood River, OR 97031. 503-386-2333.

Crater Lake Lodge Company, P.O. Box 97, Crater Lake, 97604. 503-594-2511.

Crater Lake National Park, P.O. Box 7, Crater Lake, OR 97604. 503-594-2211.

Detroit Ranger Station, HC 73, Box 320, Mill City, OR 97360. 503-854-3366.

Eagle Cap Ranger District, P.O. Box M, Joseph, OR 97828. 503-426-3104.

Florence Chamber of Commerce, 270 US 101, Florence, OR 97439. 503-997-3128.

Friends of Opal Creek, 503-897-2921.

Hart Mountain National Antelope Refuge, P.O. Box 111, Lakeview, OR 97630. 503-947-3315.

Hells Canyon National Recreation Area Headquarters, P.O. Box 490, Enterprise, OR 97828. 503-426-4978.

Hells Canyon National Recreation Area, P.O. Box 699, Clarkston, WA 99403. 509-758-0616.

John Day Fossil Beds National Monument, 420 West Main Street, John Day, OR 97845. 503-575-0721. Cant Ranch Visitor Center at Sheep Rock is 503-934-2801.

Klamath Basin NWRs, Refuge Manager, Route 1, Box 74, Tulelake, CA 96134. 916-667-2231.

Klamath County Visitors Association, P.O. Box 1867, Klamath Falls, OR 97601. 503-884-0666.

Klamath Wildlife Area, 1800 Miller Island Road West, Klamath Falls, OR 97603. 503-883-5734.

Lake County Chamber of Commerce, 513 Center Street, Lakeview, OR 97630. 503-947-6040.

Lava Lands Visitor Center, 1645 US 20 East, Bend, OR 97701. 503-382-5668.

Lewis and Clark National Wildlife Refuge, c/o Willapa National Wildlife Refuge, Ilwaco, WA 98624. 206-484-3482.

Lowell Ranger Station, Lowell, OR 97452. 503-937-2129.

Madras Chamber of Commerce, 197 S.E. 5th Street, Madras, OR 97741. 503-475-6975.

Malheur Field Station, HC 72, Box 260, Princeton, OR 97721. 503-493-2629.

Malheur National Wildlife Refuge, HC 72, Box 245, Princeton, OR 97721. 503-493-2612.

Maupin Chamber of Commerce, P.O. Box 220, Maupin, OR 97037. 503-395-2599.

Mount Hood National Forest, 2955 N.W. Division, Gresham, OR 97030. 503-666-0771.

Nature Conservancy, 1234 N.W. 25th, Portland, OR 97210. 503-228-9561.

North Bend Information Center, 1380 Sherman, North Bend, OR 97459. 503-756-4613 or 800-824-8486.

Oregon Department of Fish and Wildlife, 2501 S.W. First, Portland, OR 97207. 503-229-5403.

Oregon Dunes National Recreation Area, 855 Highway Avenue, Reedsport, OR 97467. 503-271-3611.

Oregon State Parks Campsite Information Center, 800-452-5687 inside Oregon; 503-238-7488 in Portland and outside Oregon.

Oregon State Parks, 525 Trade Street S.E., Salem, OR 97310. 503-378-6305 or 800-452-5687.

Siuslaw National Forest, 4077 S.W. Research Way, Corvallis, OR 97333. 503-757-4480.

Umatilla National Wildlife Refuge, U.S. Post Office Building, 6th and "I" Streets, Umatilla, OR 97882-0239. 503-922-3232.

Wallowa Valley Ranger District, Route 1, Box M, Enterprise, OR 97846. 503-432-2171.

Wallowa-Whitman National Forest, P.O. Box 907, Baker, OR 97814. 503-523-6391.

Western Oregon National Wildlife Refuge Complex, 26208 Finley Refuge Road, Corvallis, OR 97333. 503-757-7236.

Willamette National Forest, 211 East Seventh Avenue, Eugene, OR 97440. 503-465-6521.

Willamette National Forest, P.O. Box 907, Baker, OR 97814. 503-523-6391.

Bibliography

Armstrong, Chester H. *History of the Oregon State Parks, 1917–1963*. Salem: Oregon State Parks Commission, 1963. Uncopyrighted.

Friedman, Ralph. *In Search of Western Oregon*. Caldwell, Idaho: The Caxton Printers, 1990.

Jackman, E. R. and Long, R. A. *The Oregon Desert*. Caldwell, Idaho: The Caxton Printers, 1967.

Schaffer, Jeffrey P. and Selters, Andy. *The Pacific Crest Trail: Oregon and Washington* Vol. 2. Berkeley: Wilderness Press, 1990.

Sullivan, William L. *Exploring Oregon's Wild Areas*. Seattle: The Mountaineers, 1988.

Wallowa Resource Council. *Hiking the High Wallowas*. Edited by Frank Conley. Enterprise, OR: Pika Press, 1988.

Warren, Stuart and Ishikawa, Ted Long. *Oregon Handbook*. Chico, CA: Moon Publications, 1991.

Williams, Paul M. *Oregon Coast Hikes*. Photography by Bob and Ira Spring. Seattle: The Mountaineers, 1985.

Wood, Wendell. *A Walking Guide to Oregon's Ancient Forests*. Portland: The Oregon Natural Resources Council/Seattle: The Mountaineers, 1991.

WPA Writers Project. *Oregon: End of the Trail*. Washington, D.C.: Government Printing Office, 1940.

Index